The path we were designed to take,
may be one no else has followed.
- Lee Palmer

# ANSWERED PRAYERS WHILE YOU WERE OUT

An Aneurysm Survivor's Story
combined with

# *FAITH, HOPE & LOVE*

# DEDICATION

To my husband Marvin Palmer, my very own treasure box from heaven, whose priceless treasures I continue to experience each and every day.

To my parents Lloyd and Josephine whose continuous guidance and support have lined my life reinforcing that in the quest for excellence there is no finish line; as all things are possible if I only believe.

To my beloved sister Danielle, my very own cheerleader who always believed and supported my dreams no matter how unrealistic they may seem.

And to God ~ The One who Answered all my Prayers.

Blessings,

Lee Palmer

*"If one dream should fall and break into a thousand
pieces, never be afraid to pick
one of those pieces up and begin again" ~ Flavia
Weedn*

---

*"The Lord sitteth on the flood;
yea, the Lord sitteth King; forever.
The Lord will give strength unto his people;
the Lord will bless his people with peace."
(Psalm 29:10-11)*

# ACKNOWLEDGEMENTS

First and foremost I have to thank my Heavenly Father, the Lord of my life, my everything that I need at any given time, for giving me the wisdom, knowledge and understanding in writing this book. For entrusting me to share our story of His glory and miracle working power with the world. Thank you for your unfaltering, love, mercy and grace towards us.

I am totally indebted to my wonderful husband Marvin Palmer, the Love of my life, my best friend, my strong tower, my King created and designed just for me. One whom God has given a second chance and whom I am blessed with to accompany me on this journey with its many facets and intricacies called "LIFE". Thank you my love, for your love, patience, and continuous support.

Special thanks to Satnarine, my sister at heart whom God gave me in a covenant of friendship, my prayer partner, my other best friend. Your unwavering belief in me and continuous support over the years is unfathomable. Thank you for crying when I didn't know how, praying when I couldn't find the words and most importantly standing on your faith when I'm down and out while making room so that I can stand too.

Many thanks to our Bishop, Bishop William D. Hutchinson who has never left our side and whose spiritual guidance provided an anchor in many turbulent times; members of our church family, other family members and friends whose faith and prayers kept us through. May heaven bless you all for all you have done and each time you petitioned the throne on our behalf.

Thank you.

# Table of Contents


Chapter i.................................................... 11

When your world falls apart taking…all your hopes & dreams with it

Chapter ii................................................... 21

You called me out…into the great Unknown

Chapter iii ................................................. 31

Elevating your faith where there is no room for doubt as…… Everything depends on it

Chapter iv ................................................. 39

What to do…when you just don't know what to do

Chapter v .................................................. 51

Launching out...even if it's into the Unknown

Chapter vi ................................................. 57

Hope….A word that has no Limits

Chapter vii ................................................ 63

Finding God & clinging to Him…even in the Unknown

Chapter viii .............................................. 75

When you thought your world caved in…then the wind came & threatened what Remained

Chapter ix ................................................ 89

Living by God's leading…the journey continues at Home

Chapter x.................................................. 101

Angels all around…

Chapter xi ................................................. 109

Trusting & understanding God…in the cold, dark, Abyss

Chapter xii ...................................................................119

The Key to waiting with Endurance…

Chapter xiii ..................................................................129

The Wait…

Chapter xiv ..................................................................141

Beyond the Wait…

# Table of Contents


Chapter i ............................................................... 11

When your world falls apart taking…all your hopes &
dreams with it

Chapter ii .............................................................. 21

You called me out…into the great Unknown

Chapter iii ............................................................. 31

Elevating your faith where there is no room for doubt as……
Everything depends on it

Chapter iv ............................................................. 39

What to do…when you just don't know what to do

Chapter v .............................................................. 51

Launching out…even if it's into the Unknown

Chapter vi ............................................................. 57

Hope….A word that has no Limits

Chapter vii ............................................................ 63

Finding God & clinging to Him…even in the Unknown

Chapter viii ........................................................... 75

When you thought your world caved in…then the wind
came & threatened what Remained

Chapter ix ............................................................. 89

Living by God's leading…the journey continues at Home

Chapter x ............................................................. 101

Angels all around…

Chapter xi ............................................................ 109

Trusting & understanding God…in the cold, dark, Abyss

Chapter xii ...................................................................119

The Key to waiting with Endurance…

Chapter xiii .................................................................129

The Wait…

Chapter xiv .................................................................141

Beyond the Wait…

# When your world falls apart taking…all your hopes & dreams with it

THURSDAY MAY 28, 2015 is a day that will forever be engraved in my mind. We got up our usual time and did our morning routine which included prayer, breakfast, you hurrying me to get ready and in the end deciding to drop me at work as, as usual, I was running late. You dropped me off, we said our usual goodbyes with a smile and wished each other a blessed day as we both knew that our work days got pretty hectic this time of the month. Then it all began a series of unforgettable dramatic events that changed our lives forever.

I was sitting at my desk and had just uploaded a payroll when my cell phone rang. It was from your workplace and after the usual formalities, your Supervisor said you were not well and they had to take you over to the Doctor's office. She was relatively calm but for some reason my heart started racing and although you were just being taken for a checkup I began feeling very disturbed. I remember calling and asking my co-worker for a drive as you had kept the car that morning after you dropped me at work and the car would have been in the parking lot by now. Without further ado, I took up my handbag and flashed out of the office leaving everything as they were. Little did I know that it would be a month before I would return to my desk and to work. When I got to the Doctor's office I was led in and I saw two of your work colleagues who accompanied you, sitting in the waiting area. I then asked them where you were and after being told, I found you sitting resting your head in the palm of your hands. I rushed to your side and stooped before you saying "hun what's wrong?" After which you said "my head" and showed me the left side behind your eye.

When the Doctor came into the examination room where we were, he explained to me that you were having severe headaches but he could not understand the intensity and the disorientation that was associated with it. As he explained to me that during the length of his observation at no point did the pain lessen in its intensity. I felt the cold sweat of fear begin to clutch at me but I brushed it aside and the only time it hit me that something was terribly wrong was when he asked you where you worked and what was your date of birth. None of which you could remember or answer at the time. I went outside with tears streaming down my face and walked right into our best man who was also a work colleague of yours. He managed to calm me down and told me that you only needed some time to rest as something similar had happened to him in the past and after getting some time off to recuperate he was fine.

He then went into the examination room to speak to you and I was so happy for that, as I knew I had to regain my composure before entering the examination room once more. By then, your niece who admired you so much arrived and I showed her where you were and upon greeting her you hugged her as usual and she sat waiting with us for you to be called in once more. We were then called by the Doctor, who told me that he was going to give you a pain killer injection and that should ease the pain, and that we should let it "kick in" for a while and see what happened. It was at this point I called my mom who was a Pastor and told her to pray, she said she was nearby and would be heading over to the Doctor's office. I also called our Deaconess at our local church who happened to be your sister-in-law and told her to get the message out as urgent prayer was needed a.s.a.p.

When the Doctor returned, you were less disoriented and were able to state your date of birth though still unable to say where you worked. The Doctor being very concerned about this said he wanted to send you to a hospital nearby for observation. This I politely refused by asking what are my other options. He then said the other option is to have a brain scan done immediately and this could be done at another hospital a few parishes away.  Again I asked my options and he said ok the fastest way is to do one privately. He told me about having one done in Manchester which is actually an adjoining parish to ours, and upon making a few calls I found a place where the scan could be done immediately. A few weeks later I found out that as God would have it, I heard Manchester but he had in fact said Winchester, which is a medical complex in Kingston, a few parishes away in another direction.

As you seemed relatively calm and even walked out of the Doctor's office, stood beside me while I settled the bill etc. persons were more or less a bit settled in their mind, but deep down I was silently praying, as though you were calm you were still unable to say the colour of your shirt when the Doctor asked while writing up the referral.  In fact your response was to turn to me while saying "I don't understand what he is asking".

I took the referral and arranged with my dad to return my co-worker's car and our best man brought our car from the parking lot for me to drive.  After speaking to a few persons we left the Doctor's office as by then my parents, a few of your coworkers and your brother had arrived. With that being the case, we got in the car and left to get the scan done.  As I was told by the Doctor that I should get something for you to eat as you hadn't had lunch yet, I decided to get something on the way. I also decided to pick up your health card which I figured was at home as I headed in that direction to collect the lunch which I had asked someone from work to order for me.

With arrangements made for my mom to meet us at our house and drive us into Mandeville which is the capital of Manchester, I left out, collected the lunch and upon arriving home gave you something to eat. After having roughly a quarter to a half of it, you went to lay down while I searched for the health card. I was so nervous I began shaking and knew at the rate I was going I would never find it. It was after standing in the room and asking God to show me where it was, as I was so on edge that I found it in one of your pockets. The same pocket I searched over and over to no avail just seconds earlier. By the time I found it, my mom came and I woke you up twice as we had to go. I knew you were tired and if you had it your way you would probably want to sleep for a while but all that was going through my mind was that the quicker we get this scan done the sooner all our fears will be eliminated and we will be back home. On our way out, at the gate as a matter of fact, we saw Bishop and his wife who stopped by and wished us well on our journey.

Heading into Mandeville I sat beside you and watched you with a keen eye. I even asked the colour of your shirt and although you said green which was the right answer and of which I was relieved, there was a calmness about you that made me a bit nervous. I kept telling myself it was a result of the pain medication and when I realized your phone kept ringing and your answers were very vague I then suggested that you turn the phone off for a while, to which you agreed. After which you held my hand as mom drove us to Mandeville as quickly and safely as possible.

When we arrived at our destination, the rain was pouring like crazy. As there were many buildings on the complex and I was unsure of where I was going, I ran in the rain to the building I assumed was the one; God was so good that it was in fact the Imaging Centre and I just knew He led me to the right door since time was of essence. I then explained my situation to the receptionist who told me due to the inclement weather the machines more than likely were switched off and if they were then I would have to come back another day. I silently pleaded to God to let them be on as I had no idea what we would do as the scans had to be done immediately. I explained to her once more all that was happening and that I was to call the Doctor with the results as soon as possible.

After making some calls she said okay and I borrowed her umbrella to get you from my mom's vehicle. After getting you inside and completing the registration process, we sat beside each other holding hands as we waited. It was at this point you told me you were tired and rested your head on my shoulder. When your name was called they took us into a room with a lot of machines and showed you where to lie down and I was politely asked to step outside. Blinded by tears I left the room for what felt like an eternity. When you finally came out, I told the gentleman as I had told the receptionist that I had to call the Doctor with the results immediately and he said "ok."

After waiting a while instead of giving us the results and letting me call the Doctor, I was told the Doctor on site was in office and wanted to see me, we waited some more, then a lady came out who I later learnt was the Doctor on site, and introduced herself. We then got up to walk to the direction of her office when to my dismay she exclaimed "He can walk?!" After hearing her exclamation I had a funny feeling in my stomach and knew I was not going to like what I was about to hear.

Once we were in her office she hurriedly made you sit and brought your scan up on a screen, looked at me and explained "this is your husband's scan" and her next words literally were "this area here we are looking at is bleeding in the brain", there was total silence in the office as my heart dropped, my entire world collapsed and I heard you vaguely saying to me "I don't understand what she is saying" "what is she saying?" I took your hand, calmed you down and willed myself not to faint. I tried not to think on the fact that she is speaking and you were not understanding. All I knew was that if there is bleeding presently in the brain at no point should you get flustered or agitated as this would only make matters worse. I then took a deep breath and mustered up enough strength to stay focused on what was happening and faintly said "okay what's next?" She looked at me, took a deep breath and in terms of the way forward as it related to getting further medical assistance, said "one question.......public or private?" Without hesitation I said "private", as I saw your entire life and my entire future flash before my eyes. As I knew in this very room this very instant the answer I gave to that question would have a major impact on your survival as you needed urgent medical attention and you needed it immediately.

There is something that happens in a believer's life when their world shifts on its axis. Especially if that shift causes everything to crumble taking with it everything you have ever known including your hopes and dreams. When this shift happens, immediately you are faced with two decisions, one is to literally panic, let the tears overflow, throw in the towel by thinking this is it. The other option, is to remain calm, keep the tears in check and remind yourself that you are not alone as God is there with you. It's also in times like these you will realize that doubt and fear, along with faith and courage live on the same avenue in your heart. You just have to know which path you will take and the door you will find yourself at and keep knocking on.

I found myself at that place in my Christian walk. A place where I realized that in a matter of minutes I was so weak that I felt as if I didn't have any energy to fight. A place where doubts and fears began flooding my mind with little flecks of faith and courage bobbing to stay afloat; I just wanted to curl up and cry. I felt just like a child watching a crystal globe fall and smash into pieces, watching in horror as the water and crystals on the inside that once made it so beautiful, run out, leaving behind nothing but shards of glass. It was here that I realized that I could not do this on my own. I needed to tap into my "inner man", who is the Holy Spirit, my comforter that lives within me. More than anything I wanted to cry, throw a tantrum and get hysterical as I couldn't believe this was happening but instead, I remained focused as I knew my every move had a major impact on your survival. My aim was to keep you calm and the only way to do that was to be calm myself. It's ironic that although I knew I had to, I could barely keep calm. I began feeling light headed, as if someone knocked the lights out of me and as I struggled to find strength I could literally hear my heart pounding in sheer panic and at one point I was sure I would just pass out. But God kept me as I literally began feeling God's strength being made perfect when I am weak (2 Corinthians 12 vs 9).

# You called me out…into the great Unknown

AS WE sat waiting for the referral to take to the hospital in the same seat where we sat before we did the scan, your next words were: "this means I can't go home?" Little did I know that these were the last words I would hear for months said in that lovely smooth baritone voice. I answered your question by saying "no" and I saw a single tear roll down your cheek. That was enough to cut me to the core and right then and there in the waiting area I began talking to God as I had to make it resolute in my mind that God is with us, we will get us through this and soon you will be home.

By then things started to go by in a flurry as the letters were prepared for us to go to a nearby Hospital. In the same interim, another Doctor called saying to take you to another Hospital which was a good distance away. Apparently considering the urgency of the situation, the medical field was on high alert, and he was contacted when they could not get the one you were referred to. This Doctor was looking at an emailed copy of your scan as we spoke on the phone and just as with the Doctor who I had just spoken to, I could hear in his voice that it was not looking good.

Finally the referral was ready and we got the letter and headed out. By this time my mom came into the building looking for us as we were in there for quite some time. We headed off to the hospital with mom at the wheel and me being in my usual position at your side holding your hand. At this point, there is no way anyone could have told me that things would or even could get worse. Low and behold as we were journeying on I only felt when you gripped my hand in the back of the jeep and said "Jesus!" I then relived what happened next in my mind so many times.

I watched in horror as your head started turning to the right and it turned so much my initial thought was for fear that your neck would break. I grabbed you and started praying immediately and I prayed and I prayed and when it didn't stop I began praying in another language (praying in tongues) and when I felt nothing happening I began praying in an even deeper tongue I never even knew I had. This manifestation of the Holy Spirit - speaking in tongues is mentioned in Acts 2: 4-6 and is evident upon the initial baptism or infilling of the Holy Spirit. It is also defined by many as their "heavenly language", a language that is used directly with our Heavenly Father.  I remember saying "oh no, not my husband",  I didn't have time to cry or panic I got so upset in my spirit and got so mad at the enemy that  I literally felt as if I could just punch him in the face. I just kept praying and praying then throughout all this I saw your hand begin to curl and then you hunched over. The next thing I knew you started stretching out across my lap and it was at that point I screamed for my mom to stop the jeep and I opened the door allowing you to stretch all the way across as I remembered thinking 'he is tall and he cannot bump his head as there is a bleed somewhere in there'.

I remember hearing mommy say "Lord all I have in my hand is water" and she started pleading the blood of Jesus and splashing us with a bottle of water she had in her hand. Later on I realized she was referring to a famous scripture she always took comfort in, Exodus 4:2 the one where God asked Moses *what is that in thy hand?"* This He asked Moses when Moses did not know what to do when he was sent to Pharoah to free the children of Israel.  The response to this question was *"a rod"* as God was reinforcing the point that whatever you have in your hand use it. This was the very same staff that was used in scriptures in the Bible where God's miraculous wonders were performed. One such wonder, was in the parting the Red Sea where Moses lead the people out of bondage, their enemies were behind them, the Red Sea before them and mountains on the other side, here the sea parted making a way out of no way for Moses and the children of Israel (Exodus 14).

I later learnt by the medical professionals, that you had a seizure due to the bleeding in the brain. Once the seizure subsided you slumped onto me lifeless, totally lifeless and once again I did not have any time to panic as I realized that I had to fight and this time the battle was not only in the physical but spiritual as well. You were no longer able to fight for yourself and I made up in my mind and purposed in my heart that you shall not die. I grabbed you around the chest, searched for the faintest heart beat and began speaking to your heart as I willed it to continue beating. I remember earlier on in our marriage you would smile and shake your head as I spoke to everything whether organs, insects or animals I had the habit of saying "go away" or "mosquito leave me alone" and this time was no different. I spoke to your heart like another human being I told it to keep on beating, never to give up, never to give in. This I kept on doing as deep down I knew that there is power in the spoken word. I even remember hearing mommy say keep him awake and don't let his tongue roll back. I had no clue what she was saying but I began calling your name and when I said "it's Lesa" twice I heard you say a faint "hmm?" this I kept doing while she drove to the hospital as fast as she could.

When we got to the hospital, she was the first one out of the jeep as she ran inside for a wheelchair that they tried to get you in, by this you were barely conscious if conscious any at all and after they wheeled you into a room, the nurse began calling for another porter to assist in getting you on the bed, a porter who could not be found. Seeing the urgency of the situation as you had to be placed on a bed I rolled up my sleeves and said "look I will lift him if I have to as there is no porter around and I am not going to wait on the other one to arrive". Seeing my determination she said "no that's okay" and then lifted you to the bed with the assistance of the porter who was there. At this point you began struggling to move and I wondered if you were going into shock and after restraining you, they began the "stabilizing process" as I was told. I stood in horror with tears streaming down my face as on came all the tubes, wires and gadgets from IV to oxygen to all kind of different things and all I could think of was how deathly pale you looked and that you were not moving any at all. It was then I continued saying in my mind "no not my husband" and I said it over and over as I watched in horror as nurses and Doctors ran to and from your side fighting to save your life. They then asked us to give them a minute and while they did their thing I began filling out forms you name it to have you transferred to another hospital. This I had to do as they said you had to see a Neurosurgeon as soon as possible. Hearing those words resonating in my ear, made my knees go weak as I knew Neuro had to do with the nervous system in this particular instance the brain and Surgeon in itself is self-explanatory. Somewhere in the midst of it all we contacted our Bishop to give him an update on what was happening and he arrived with his wife and your brother. Both Bishop and his wife began praying earnestly, this they did while your brother, unable to contain all that was happening broke down in tears at one end of the room. Bishop's wife prayed in tongues right through and all I could do was stand with silent tears running down my cheeks repeating "not my husband not my husband". I refused to see what was staring me right in the face as you were no longer responsive and you were attached to so many different machines.

While I was in the office finalizing the paperwork a million and one thoughts filled my mind. Not only were Doctors calling me as they wanted you to be their patient. I was also faced with the reality that if I did not settle your bill the ambulance would remain in that fixed position and never leave the compound. That was a thought I did not have the time to entertain as you had to be rushed immediately to another hospital in another parish, where the neurosurgeon was. After being told that health insurance would not cover the bill as you were not an "in patient" I also realized that the real urgency lie in me. As God would have it a few months ago I took home an application form for a Pre-Approved Credit Card with this fairly new bank. After promising you that it would only be used in case of an emergency you had given me the go ahead to get it. As I sat there I said to myself it is a good thing I remained true to my promise and I silently prayed that it would work as it had never been used. I held my breath as I handed over the card and watched it being swiped and after a few minutes I breathed a sigh of relief as I heard the paper in the Credit Card machine being printed for me to sign. I then signed and whispered a silent thank you to the most High God.

Finally after settling the bill the ambulance was geared up and ready to go and they wheeled you out on a stretcher. At the same time Bishop explained to me that I may not be allowed to go with you in the ambulance, but I could follow in a vehicle behind. Later Bishop told me he was happy I didn't see when they placed you in the ambulance as when the nurse tubed you, you didn't even budge and usually once that is done with the oxygen the normal reaction is for your body to move in a jerking motion. When I got outside and saw you in the ambulance stretched out on your back I touched your feet and I remembered thinking they were oh so cold. I knew I might not be able to travel in the ambulance with you as Bishop had reminded me of that fact but after touching your feet I wasn't so sure I wanted you to go alone. They then closed the ambulance doors, turned on the flashing lights and the siren and sped off. Whether it was the siren, the flashing lights, the speed they took off with or the fact that I was no longer with you, something happened right then and there, it was like reality settled in. With it came the tears I had been holding at bay and they began falling nonstop. I then began crying hysterically, right then and there in the parking lot as I literally felt as if my heart was ripped out. I remembered hearing someone wailing then realizing the sound was coming from my own lips.  I remember your brother holding me, then shaking me, I even remember vaguely Bishop's wife saying "get her in a vehicle", and somewhere in the distance I heard my mother  saying "Lesa, Lesa its mommy listen to me it's ok to cry but you have to calm down".  I know I was given some water to drink and was placed to lay down in my mom's jeep and from then on the journey to another parish miles away began, mommy at the wheel, your brother in the front passenger seat and myself shuddering in the back seat. Midway when we stopped for gas at the gas station, I began to panic as on top of everything my phone battery died and my number was the only contact the hospital had. Fortunately God stepped in once more and Bishop lent us his cell phone car charger, this he gave me when we parted ways with me promising to keep them updated as they headed home and we took the toll road to what awaited us in Kingston.

30

# Elevating your faith where there is no room for doubt as...... Everything depends on it

THE JOURNEY to the hospital seemed forever and once again a million and one questions filled my mind. It was here, on my mother's passenger seat at the back that once more reality settled in as I made a stark realization that hope, faith, doubt and fear all live on the same avenue in our hearts. In fact the avenue is one in such where the houses are semidetached and you have to really ensure that you choose the right house as if you make the wrong stop you may end up knocking on the wrong door. Fear and doubts are emotions that can create havoc with one's emotional wellbeing; as it has a numbing effect on an individual because it erases faith and hope. As I lay on that back seat watching the vehicles go by journeying to their various destinations I decided to make my final destination that of hope and faith; as they in turn erase all doubts and fears, all I needed to do was remain positive.

When we finally got to the hospital and I was led to

your room I was filled with joy and sadness. A weird combination but that was exactly how I felt. Joy because you were alive and I could see your heart rate on one of the various monitors to your right. Sadness because you were so pale and lifeless, in fact you didn't even know we were there. I had no idea what stabilized meant at the time but the nurse told me you were being kept stabilized. The only thing that mattered to me was that your heart was still beating.  It was then I met your Neurosurgeon, a very calm individual with a reassuring persona and he explained to me that the following day a detailed brain scan called an angiogram will have to be done. He said an appointment could be made for 1:00 p.m. and that I should head home and get some rest. We would then meet at the location where you will be doing the angiogram the following day as you would be taken by ambulance. Around the same time the Doctor in Mandeville where we had the initial scan done called to check up on you, and after giving her an update she was a bit hesitant in her response as she figured the earliest an angiogram was done the better. In fact she wanted it done the very same night; but that was not possible.

My mom stayed with me that night, or morning rather as after we dropped your brother home it was 3:00 a.m.

Neither of us slept that morning as we whispered prayers and urgently waited for day break. Later that morning before we headed to Kingston I called one of your close friends, who so happened to be in Jamaica, informing him of the previous day's events. He inquired about where I was and as he did not have his car, he told me to come and meet him before heading in to see you. When we turned on his road we saw him walking hastily to meet us as he had a business engagement but wanted to see me first. Then and there he gave me an envelope with Fifty Thousand Dollars (J$50,000) and said I should take it with me as we don't know what lies ahead. I took it with heartfelt gratitude and tears in my eyes as such a thoughtful gesture had to come from someone who allowed themselves to be used by God as He alone knew what was ahead of us. When we got to Kingston, while making the appointment for the angiogram at around 10:00 a.m. your Neurosurgeon called saying I should not make a payment as yet as they had to get you in an ambulance and get you there a.s.a.p. as your vitals were dropping.

My heart literally dropped and once more my world capsized this time a wave of nausea swept over me as the cold fingers of fear slowly gripped my heart. I remember being led to a waiting room and sitting beside my mom, I don't even remember the direction we took to get there or even remember sitting, but all I know I was there. The longer I waited the more nervous I became and when I couldn't see the ambulance arriving with you I called the Doctor and he said he would have to call me back as he was with you. I thought he meant you had arrived and he was in the room with you, but a lady came in the waiting area and asked me if I heard anything else as you should have arrived by now and that's when I realized you weren't there as yet.

While we waited mom took up her usual position of reading her little bible that she carried around in her pocket book. This she normally does whenever she is seated waiting. She tried everything to get me to remain seated but I could not. In fact I couldn't even keep still, the only thing I could do was silently pray that you were alive. I stood at the glass window fighting once again to keep the tears at bay as I waited and waited to hear a siren.

In the meantime my phone kept ringing as Doctors from all over the island wanted you as their patient. One literally told me not to let your Neurosurgeon do a surgery if that was needed as I would regret it as he is the best.  I sat with tears streaming down my face as I did not know what to do. Here was a doctor with you fighting to save your life and here was another insisting that he was the best. In the end I remember the words of my mother "Whenever you feel the world is closing in, do what Jesus did and find a quiet place to pray". Right then and there I sat in that waiting room pasted on the window and I said "God I know nothing about Neurosurgeons and anything of this magnitude, please select the right doctor for my husband, as I don't know what to do and my eyes are fixed on you". I don't know how long I prayed for or how long I zoned out in total despair but after what seemed like an hour I got a phone call that they were on the way with you. A little from that I finally heard an ambulance and then another, I remember thinking I was never so happy to hear a siren in my life. When the second  ambulance pulled up I just knew you were in that one.  Then the wait continued as they began running the various scans, during this time your brother arrived. We sat there the three of us each in our own world connected by our faith and held together by hope and love.

After around an hour the same lady who had asked me earlier if I had heard anything, rushed out to me and said based on the results of the first angiogram they needed to do another, this one for six vessels or something to that effect of which I said "ok". That was when I saw you, when you were being wheeled on a stretcher to the other room for a more in depth scan. Tears filled my eyes as you were just there quite oblivious to everything with a host of doctors and nurses surrounding you and giving orders as they fought to save your life.  I looked at your brother and he hugged me with tears in his eyes, I looked over to mom and she was watching me and I could tell she was silently praying I would not break down in tears. It was at this time I heard someone say to me "you have been doing good Mrs. Palmer, don't break down now". It was the voice of one of the ladies who worked there and after saying that she rushed into the room where they took you.

The duration of this scan was much longer that the first and I began to wonder if you would be strong enough to endure both scans in such quick succession. However as the little niggling thoughts of doubts and fear tried to creep in I kept telling myself you were ok and all will be well. When the scan was finished, a lady who was very supportive asked if I got the chance to see you and I told her I only caught a glimpse of you when you were moved to the other room. She then said I could see you for just a minute. As we headed to where you were, in the area where the ambulance would pick you up, she began prepping me about you not looking like yourself etc. and I realized she was afraid I would break down.

When I saw you, you appeared to be sleeping and although very pale I knew you were alive. You were surrounded by doctors and two huge men like bodyguards who seemed to be prepared to pounce on me if I panicked and tried to create a scene. Seeing that you were alive gave me renewed hope and I kissed you on your forehead and stepped back as I knew they had to move with you immediately. I was then taken to the reception area and this was where I watched in amazement as God began working in mysterious ways, showing and reminding me that He was with me and that He will never leave me nor forsake me (Deuteronomy 31:8).

As I was being led to the reception area, I was given some forms to fill out and with no delay was told that the cost of your scans was Three Hundred and Sixty Thousand Dollars (J$360,000), my eyes widened in sheer panic, which I quickly dismissed. When I was called to the receptionist, I sat down while she quoted the figure once more to me and I said okay, opened my handbag and took out a pen. Looking back I realized I had no idea what I was doing as I did not have that money nor did I own a cheque book so taking out a pen would be irrelevant. Afterwards someone said to me, although I didn't have a cheque book God had one for me and for that I am eternally grateful. So there I was sitting before these people having no idea how I would be able to settle this debt, one I had to settle quickly and return to the hospital to meet with the doctor and hear the scan results. I took a deep breath and with pen in hand I looked up and the receptionist said "oh hold on he has a health insurance policy. Let me work out the amount, I don't even have to await confirmation just pay Seventy Thousand Dollars (J$70,000)". I smiled as I tried to quiet my heart and calm down as all I had in my bag was Seventy Thousand (J$70,000) on a credit card, not a dollar more nor a dollar less and I said thank you Jesus! You are indeed an awesome wonder!

# Chapter iv

# What to do…when you just don't know what to do

WHEN I arrived at the hospital I was anxious to hear the scan results, but nothing prepared me for what was to come. Mom and I met your doctor in the parking lot and right then and there, a life changing decision had to be made. While he began taking out various apparatus from his vehicle and giving a wave of instructions to hospital staff, I was told that you did not have one problem as he initially thought but the in depth scan revealed a total of three problems. Apart from the ruptured blood vessel, there was also a massive clot formed as a result and the size of this clot had quadrupled overnight. Along with that there was another vessel at the risk of rupturing anytime soon as a result of the size of the clot. I was also informed that they would have to go in immediately and do major life saving brain surgery, an emergency craniotomy in fact. All in hopes of saving your life as at this point in time you were slipping in and out of consciousness. We listened in total shock and when we thought that was the bad part, it got even worse as we were then told that the surgery would take me anywhere from Ten to Thirteen Million Dollars (J$10,000,000 - J$13,000,000). Right then and there I decided that even if it means selling everything we own including the very clothes on my back, the surgery had to be done as you shall not die. I preferred to start life all over again with you than to continue life without you. As your doctor spoke I whispered a silent prayer to the most high and I said "God I am asking you to pay this one for me". I kept saying over and over "he shall not die" and after a brief discussion he then told me that a twelve hour surgery will then be on its way and immediately I should get you registered.

I was then led to the Administration Office where I began the registration process, which meant coming up with the initial deposit of Two Hundred and Fifty Thousand Dollars (J$250,000). Looking back I am filled with awe at how God took me through the entire process. I was first told that usually persons would not have been given a bed unless they had been registered. As you arrived after the office was closed this was not the case and you got a bed and the nurses and doctors took the utmost care of you; ensuring they did their part in keeping you alive. I filled out forms after forms while thinking of every possible means of where I would find the money to register you. I then decided to try and access our bank accounts from my phone, this proved a difficult task as the connection on the mobile data was very poor. Eventually I got on and began pulling funds from every account accessible to me to pay the deposit while struggling to remain calm throughout the entire process.

God is indeed a good God as the first One Hundred Thousand (J$100,000) came from my parents, as without hesitation my mom said "take this card your dad and I have a Hundred Thousand on it". I then prayed for the data plan on my phone to continue working as I called my dad explaining that apart from the money my mom just gave, I am going to have to practically empty his bank accounts and his words to me are words I will never forget as he told me to do what I have to do as this is a life and death situation. I then began transferring funds online as fortunately I had access to his accounts. At this time I vaguely remember the lady in the office saying take your time, I am calling the kitchen for some mint tea for you and your mom as she realized that my Thursday ran right into my Friday and I could only imagine how pale and frantic I looked.

After sitting in sheer panic wondering what to do as I was still falling short I remembered a few months ago a very close friend of mine overseas wanted to do something nice for us and she said she was sending some money for us to have a weekend away for even two nights at a hotel. This she decided to do as she thought a break would be nice as we both had recently lost family members who were close to us in a short span of time.  After contacting our banks on numerous occasions as the amount though deducted from her account was not being reflected in mine, we were told that the transaction was not successful and the sender would have to resend the said amount. A few days after this was done to my dismay the amount was reflected in my account twice and I ended up getting twice as much as she initially intended. We discussed it in detail and decided to wait on the bank to sort it out. Little did I know this was in the Lord's making as he knew I would be needing access to some additional funds. After a huge sigh I transferred this amount to my local account as I knew it would be taken from my account any day now and decided to call her and let her know as soon as possible.

Then and there with this last transaction the deposit was made after a myriad of transfers using three credit cards, one debit card, and the cash I had gotten from your friend. What a mighty God we serve. When I breathed a sigh of relief the lady in the office smiled and said "please now can you at least take a sip of the tea". I whispered thank you Jesus as I took my first sip. With the deposit being paid, I was taken to the doctor to fill out some additional forms and that's when I saw you, laying there looking totally lifeless. They told me I could talk to you and I held your hand and began encouraging you. In fact the only time I did not talk to you was when I had to go through all the forms I had to sign with a flurry. There was no time to mull over anything; your Doctor was the one that went through most of it with me explaining along the way and showing me where to sign. I remember saying in my mind no in the name of Jesus each time he explained the different things that could go wrong. As it was a brain surgery there was the possibility of loss of sight, speech, mobility, you name it he said it and there was always the possibility that you would remain in a coma. Each time something negative was mentioned each time I dismissed it in my mind as I told myself your surgery would be a success.

After all the paperwork was finished I was left with you for a few minutes in private. I took back my position of holding your hand and I literally pushed all negative thoughts out my head. I didn't focus on how cold your hand was, or how lifeless you looked, I didn't focus on the missed calls from the other doctor, I began speaking to your soul. I kept speaking edifying things reminding you that God is with you, that you are strong, I reminded you of everything including our future children that was prophesied to us years before. It was then and there at the mention of their names that you squeezed my hand ever so gently and I realized you heard me. Tears filled my eyes and to this day, I cannot explain the joy that filled my heart when you squeezed my hand in recognition of their names. I then prayed for you and that was how the doctors found me praying earnestly and asking God to be the one in control, to do this twelve hour brain surgery to guide every instrument, every tool and every hand. When I opened my eyes I saw that during my prayer the nurses and doctors had returned to the room and everyone was looking at me. I then kissed your forehead and walked to every single person in the room who would be operating on you and told them "God be with you". One particular individual gave me a weird look and I smiled and said to myself if you are going to be a part of this operation on my husband God has to go with you.

The fact that you squeezed my hand ever so gently fanned the flame of hope that was burning within me. It was no surprise you responded to the names of our children, you had always loved kids and it has been an earnest desire of our hearts to have children of our own. After years of battling various setbacks I had not realized it but I had begun accepting the fact that I might never have children. I would say things like "if it is to happen it will happen" and I began getting complacent believing that lie from the pit of hell.  It all began after we were married and the time came when we decided to have a family of our own. We went to a doctor who at the time the enemy used in a part of his devious scheme. There in that doctor's office I listened in total dismay as we were told that I might never fall pregnant and that even if I did chances are I would end up miscarrying. Picture a wife hearing her doctor tell her husband that this is the woman you chose to marry and this is how it is. I could not believe how cold the doctor was and at one point I was even told that one of my results would be the perfect example to show her class of what your result should never look like.  I was devastated to say the least and when we left that office little did I realize how many seeds of doubt the enemy had planted in my mind. It was when I was informed by my Doctor the following year after that diagnosis, that there was the possibility that I had miscarried that I realized how much I believed the negative report a year earlier as at that point I felt like all those negative things told to me a year ago were coming to pass.

It took serious growth in my Christianity to let me realize that it is important not to let your fears overcome your faith and that I am more than a conqueror in the name of the Lord. That I can also decree and declare a thing and watch it come to pass (Job 22:28) as the same power that raised Jesus from the dead lives in me. I began feeding on the word of God and found all the ladies in the bible that had delays conceiving, including: Elizabeth, Sarah, Hannah, Rachel and Rebecca I would then read the scriptures daily speaking positivity into our lives and into my heart. What amazed me is that these women all had miracle babies who were all Great Men of God. The more I fed on the word, the more I became encouraged and the more my faith erased my fears as I began expecting and anticipating a mighty move of God.

It was in the year 2012, God being the caring Father that He is, saw my need and in turn our fears and met us at the point of our need. It was the year we received our first prophecy from one of our Ministers regarding our children. She was my spiritual mother, counselor, mentor and friend, in fact we were the very first couple she counseled and she was always there for us. She prayed, encouraged, petitioned on our behalf and stood in the gap at every cross road we ever came across while advising us on major decisions that we had to make. In that year May 2012 to be exact, we were told to prepare for our children as I will conceive and that we should start buying some baby clothes. After receiving that word, I made plans that after work the next day I would head into town to do just that. However, during the course of the day I began to feel "off" and by the time the day was done I was terribly ill. Nonetheless I went into the store and I bought a few baby items one of my favorite was a jumper set that had "Little Miracle" written on it.

It was here at this point in my life, that I was reminded of how important it is to marry the one God ordained for you as I had no fear or worry about what you would think, say or do when you got home and saw all these things that I had purchased. In fact when you got home you were so excited to see them on our bed that it brought tears to my eyes as somehow just seeing them made our promise seem more real. You could have said

I was crazy or living in a fantasy world or make negative comments, but you didn't. I mean who buys baby clothes without confirming a pregnancy? The answer to that question is those who are willing to take a step out in faith, not only faith but crazy faith believing that preparation precedes blessings and if God said it is so then it is so as He alone has the final say.

I rushed home from the store that day to take them out and offer up praises to the most high God as at this point in my life, I was at a higher level of praise and expectancy was high in my heart. When I got home I praised God for meeting us at the point of our need by giving us a word and while singing to him I began worshiping Him. Worship from that day forward became a part of my lifestyle and one day without even realizing it I moved straight into Tehillah Praise which is a spontaneous new song straight from the melody in my heart. It is the praise that God inhabits and day by day I would sing the second time around moving straight into a Zamar Praise which is praise by speaking and making music accompanied by the voice. These are the transitions into a higher level of praise that our children would be named.

As we sat in the "family room" while your surgery began I kept thinking to myself twelve hours is a long time for an operation, especially in an area as delicate as the brain. I wondered if I made the right decision in terms of hospital and if you would be strong enough to survive a surgery now coming out of doing two angiograms. I was however determined not to let fear take over and I began speaking to my soul as I sat in the lounge chair my eyes fixated before me. The steady vibration of my phone brought me back to reality and after replying to as many calls and messages as I could I began to feel weariness of the past two days settle in. Although it was Friday my Thursday had not yet ended as the days felt as if they were combined in one. Not only was I tired, I was also feeling ill, so much so that the suggestion was made that I go to your niece's place and rest even for a few minutes. But there was no way I could leave now, and I decided to remain where I was. With my mom seated to the right beside me and your niece seated on my left, I felt a sense of gratitude. I looked ahead and saw your brother in the couch and I was so grateful for the love of family as there was no way I could have endured the next twelve hours by myself as they were the longest hours in my entire life.

# Chapter v

# Launching out...even if it's into the Unknown

IT WAS around 2:00 a.m. while we sat in the waiting room slowly dozing off, that I began seeing your eyes; almost as if in a vision. Those beautiful brown eyes, the colour and shape of almonds, were just looking at me and I sat there reminiscing of the love and laughter normally reflected in them. After a few minutes however I realized that something was wrong as I began seeing them more and more.  It was at that time I sensed in my spirit that something in relation to your eyes was not right in that operating room and there was the serious need for intercession. I immediately signaled to my mother, your niece and woke your brother informing them that we needed to go to God in prayer immediately regarding the surgery especially as it relates to the optic nerve.

This was not the first time I have seen things that needed to be dealt with urgently in the spiritual realm. The first encounter I had when I realized this gift was bestowed upon me was a few years ago at Youth Camp.

That morning while worshipping God in our time of praise I saw someone almost as if in a vision before me in tears, it was not ordinary tears but heart wrenching sobs that broke my heart. I begged God to let me help her as my heart broke at the depth of her pain. Slowly I began to see features like her hair, but for me that was not enough I wanted to know who it was so I could help her and as I pleaded with God to show me who it was He did. I left morning worship pondering what had happened and I began thinking okay I know who it is, now what? So I began praying for her believing that was all that was required, little did I know this was just the beginning. The following morning while in worship the previous day's events that I saw began playing out right before my eyes. While worshiping the said young lady walked up to me sobbing hysterically. I literally froze, then I embraced her in a tight hug, prayed for her, then handed her over to one of the counsellors that were present. It was after I returned to my local church and spoke to my Youth Minister I got some insight into what happened.  What happened was that at Youth Camp I was bestowed that morning as we worshipped with one of the gifts mentioned in 1st Corinthians 12:8, the gift of Word of Knowledge.

This is the reason why I became alert when I kept

seeing your eyes. Right then and there in that hospital family waiting room I began to intercede in ways I have never done before and ways I could never even imagine. I began praying for what was happening in the operating theatre and I began rebuking the enemy, reminding him that you have not yet laid eyes on your children so there is no way you could lose your sight. At one point I remember calling on the Archangel Michael and Gabriel for help and telling them to come with me as I am going into that operating room to war in the spirit. Then and there I was taken into another spiritual dimension, fighting battles no one else could see and more determined than ever to win as you were unable to fight for yourself. While praying in the spirit I even felt my right hand begin to move of its own will very skillfully and delicately. Looking back I realized it was if I was somehow being used along with the angels to guide the hand of the doctors as they operated on you.

By the time I was about to finish praying, I was totally exhausted and found myself on my knees praying in an unknown tongue. I prayed and I prayed until there was nothing left within me. So much so that I had to crawl on my knees to your niece and rested my head on her lap. I was totally exhausted, I felt sick to the point where it seemed as if there was little or no life left within me. After being assisted to my seat as we gave thanks for God coming through in all the areas we had prayed, we all resumed waiting anxiously for news of what was happening in the operating theatre. I was so anxious and my stomach was in knots, each time we heard footsteps in the hallway we looked anxiously expecting some news. At one point when I could not bear it any longer I went to the nurses station located nearest to the waiting room in search of any news I could find. It was then I was informed that all seems to be going well. I then ventured to my usual position of waiting and each time we heard a footstep we all fixed our eyes on the door. As the minutes turned into the remaining hours that was left of the twelfth hour and began going into the thirteenth hour I began wondering what was happening. When I was sure I would have passed out from sheer anxiety, we saw a gentleman in scrubs walking by and I ran out to ask him if he was in the operating room with you. He then replied yes and that all went well. I was so relieved I could not contain the tears from falling and a nurse then came in to inform us that it was normal for the time to go over as I did not take into consideration the preparation time before surgery. At this point we all whispered heartfelt thanks to God almighty for taking you thus far and prepared for the journey home.

The next day your Doctor greeted me and the first thing he said was "I felt your prayers", he then went on to say that your surgery was a tough one and at one point they had to stop and regroup. He also informed me that you also had a blown pupil and pointed to your eye that was swollen shut. Your brother looked up at me upon hearing this and I knew he was remembering our prayers regarding the optic nerve. My blood ran cold as the entire night events of interceding flashed before my eyes. God in His infinite wisdom stepped in right on time and the fact that intercession was made I knew your eyes would be alright. The two weeks that followed while you were in the hospital is something that I will never forget. I watched from the day you opened your eye after surgery, the process it took during recovery, to when both eyes were fully opened in total amazement. The truth is the fact that you were admitted for just two weeks was a miracle in itself as the very few who recover usually remain in the hospital for a month or more and many sad to say do not make it home.

The first time I saw you when you were awakened after surgery, your doctor and a few nurses were with you calling your name and he told me to come closer to see how you would respond to me. I knew then and there that he was actually saying, I want to see if he remembers you. I remember approaching your bedside desperately trying to find you beneath all those bandages and tubes. Then as I looked at your face I saw your one visible eye light up with that look of love you have only for me. My heart melted and tears filled my eyes as I knew that look anywhere,  that look from the day we met was reserved only for me and I had no doubt you recognized me and knew who I was.

# Hope….A word that has no Limits

WITH YOU recognizing who I was I drifted off into a happy place and came back to reality at the very moment your Doctor said "he responds to you differently which is a good sign as before he was hardly focusing on us and now he has shifted all his attention to you". He then told you to kiss me and ever so slightly your lips twitched and he smiled and said "it takes a lot of brainpower to attempt to kiss much less to smile and he is attempting to do both with you". My heart was filled with gratitude, you made it, God kept you through that twelve hour surgery and on top of that, you remembered me. I wanted to just fall to my knees and thank God for all He has done, but I knew this was not the time or the place. Instead I held your hand hidden beneath the various tubes and wires, lifted my head to the heavens and silently whispered thank you to the most high God.

The following day after stepping out of the room to let the nurses get a chance to check your vitals and administer your medication, I sat outside looking over at the mountains. I remembered then and there how amazing and all powerful our Heavenly Father really is. I looked at the building right across from your room and for the first time I realized that there was a little bird perched right at the corner of the roof. Little did I know that that little bird would be a reminder each and every day of how steadfast God's love really is. There was never a day I went to visit you that I did not see this bird, even if it was not there at first, as the evening approached it would resume its position perched on the roof. Similarly there was never a day that I came to visit you when I did not feel God's love, even when I panicked and my heart was gripped by fear and I felt so alone, He was always there.

This particular day was no different, as I sat there with your brother your Doctor came and he was extremely exhausted as he had done your surgery that spanned over two days,  kept a close eye on you immediately after, then attended a meeting in another parish earlier that day. After greeting us, he told us he was just going to check on you for a few minutes then head on home. It's amazing how when things seem to be going right that time is of no major concern, but once there is a change in events things are entirely different.  As we waited  for  your  Doctor  to  return,  the  minutes amounted to fifteen then turned into half an hour then to my dismay an hour had passed. From where I was seated outside your room, I began hearing him calling your name repetitively and urgently; at one point I even heard a thudding sound I could not explain. This went on for a few minutes, at that point I was on a call with one of my Youth Ministries Director. I told her that we had to go into prayer immediately as I don't like the urgency in which they were calling your name. I then called your brother who I could not find as the last thing I remembered was that he was with me when I got the call. When he answered I told him what I heard and he said ok he is on his way back to me. I sat back on the chair, feeling a sweep of terror roll over me like a flood and with tears streaming down my face I asked God to please spare your life. I kept thinking to myself after making it through twelve hours of surgery you just have to be alright as you have made it thus far.

When the minutes turned into another hour and there was still no sign of the doctor we decided to head on home and I went in to kiss you goodbye. That was where I found him crouched in a chair monitoring the various machines that you were connected to. As he was the one monitoring you and not the nurse I know something drastic had happened. For one, I know he was tired and the nurse was the one who usually does all the monitoring that he was doing now. With emotions constricting my throat I managed to ask if everything is ok to which he responded "your husband is very strong as he managed to pull out one of the tubes". It was seven months down the line your brother told me what he actually saw that evening.

Before I called him he had heard the Doctor calling your name and he decided to take a walk. It was at that time he realized that none of the nurses was at their station which was outside your room. As curiosity got the better of him he peeped in through the window and saw everyone including the nurses surrounding your bed and the doctor trying to revive you. He didn't know what to do or what to say, neither was he able to face me for fear of somehow disclosing too much about what he saw. This he knew would probably end up in me becoming a patient as well as he knew I was at the verge of breaking point. That was when he decided to take a walk as I received a call. He was shaken up about it so much that when he got home he placed his cell phone away in a drawer, it was loud enough for him to hear if it rang, but deep down he really did not want to receive a call from me. After witnessing what he saw he knew if I called he would fear the news I would bring. That night I laid in bed looking at the ceiling and tracing every pattern engraved there in an attempt to calm my nerves as the house felt so huge without you. It's funny how the mind works as with all the decisions that were to be made and going from one place to the other, there was no time to think about anything else but you.  Now with me being in a fixed position all the thoughts that seemed to be chasing me for the past few days, began catching up with me.  A million and one questions filled my mind and looking back I realized had it not been for the Lord on my side I have no idea where I would be.

At some point in the night I remember thinking about and asking God what about our finances? How am I going to cover the fee for the hospital and nurses? He then brought to my mind a health plan that I vaguely remembered you mentioned some time ago. I got out of bed and He led me to it, after finding it I spent the entire night looking for a clause or anything to say yes it could be used in this instance, but found none. I did not know what to do or what to think, as we usually discussed every and anything. It was at this point it finally settled in that you were not here. I couldn't say "hun do you think I could use this?"  Then and there the tears came, this time in heart wrenching sobs that could not and would not subside and that was how I spent the rest of the night, in tears while hoping your Doctor did not call and if he did it would be with good news. Early the next morning he did just that, he called and I felt as if my heart stopped beating as I watched his name appear on the Caller ID on my phone. When I answered however he was just giving me an update on what is currently happening and what to expect in terms of putting funds together for nurses, tests and various scans. I must admit God knew what he did when he chose your Doctor as he was very thorough and for one like myself who had no clue on what was next, he always gave me a heads up and let me know the next course of events. When I saw you that morning I was just so relieved to be by your side and I willed myself to get used to the various machines. I constantly reminded myself that all the beeps and various sounds they gave off were not to terrify me but they were doing their part in God's divine plan in keeping you alive. I sat and watched from your bedside in total gratitude and amazement as your emergency lifesaving surgery was over and now the recovery process had begun.

# Finding God & clinging to Him…even in the Unknown

YOUR RECOVERY and healing process had begun, and day by day I devised strategies on pushing my fear and anxiety aside as I began to look on with expectancy to experience a deeper realm of God's miracle working power in our lives. God was indeed on our side and this was evident each and every day and I was even able to get some time off work to stay with you. Day by day I came to the hospital, spoke to you, sat at your bedside and held your hand. I had devotions, read the bible, sang songs, fixed blankets, pillows you name it I did it; anything to let you feel better and keep my thoughts positive. It was also at this point in my life, I was reminded of just how loved we were. It was not just about the calls, prayers and the messages, or the various gifts in the form of plants, flowers and gift baskets. It was also about the kindness bestowed to us from the nurses, a smile from the janitor, a meal from the cafeteria everywhere I turned there we were surrounded by love.

I was convinced nurses, have a heart of care and a touch of love as they were always there showing they care. One even walked from the other end of the property to your room each and every day to say good morning. She explained her brother went through something similar and was not as fortunate as you were and that coming to tell you good morning each day made her feel better somehow. She even went further to say he was in a coma for a very long time after his surgery and when he woke up he was never the same. I remember looking into her eyes filled with tears and saying "it's never too late for a miracle" to which she smiled and said "that's so true". Moments like these left an imprint on my heart and day by day I began to see how God used you and the miracle surrounding all you had to go through to touch the lives of many.

As the days rolled by, my cousin and her wonderful husband opened up their home to me to ease the stress, strain and expense of commuting to and from Kingston to Clarendon. Not only did I have a nice place to sleep, I also had someone else looking out for me reminding me that I'm not alone. No matter how tired she was after work and attending to her little daughter she always ensured that there was dinner left for me and even sat with me while I willed each bite of food to go down in my churning stomach. It was not that I didn't know I should eat, and the food was nice and appealing to the palate, it was just that my thoughts and mind was constantly on you and if you were okay.

The days I spent in her home felt like a sanctuary or a spiritual retreat and God knew I needed just that. I would wake up in the morning to melodious singing of praise songs or prayer and knew it was time for morning worship. We would pray and praise God putting everything to Him and she would intercede for you and in turn for us in every way God taught her to. It was then and there I was reminded that as a child of God it matters not where you go, who you are with and what you have to endure, God has already assigned his angels here on earth at specific locations to minister to our needs. Even the very health plan that God led me to the night I was home all alone she assisted me in praying about. After calling and checking all around I was told there was no benefit that you could receive from it. However, I refused to give up or give in as this was the last option I had in terms of finances to carry me through the day to day expenses including paying the nurses and filling your prescriptions. In the end God led me to someone who said it was worth filling up a living benefit form and so it was one morning during morning worship as we prayed, I knelt on the same form before God and placed it in His hands. I explained the situation as it was, which is that I needed funds to pay the nurses and to take care of your daily needs. I asked Him to work it out the best way He knew how and in a way only He can and in a few months He did just that. He came through and I was able to get a portion from it to settle our day to day expenses.

As I sat at your bedside watching you sleep I realized that God is not one who slacks on His promises this He told us in 2 Peter 3:9. He also said in Deuteronomy 31:6 that He would never ever leave us nor forsake us and I felt His presence daily in that hospital room. As I was at your side each day, I got first-hand information on lab tests, reports you name it and for every result that came God kept us. Even when I realized that there was no movement in the right side of your body, though my heart raced I tried not to panic as I knew God was near and that knowledge alone calmed the raging storm within me. Although that was the case you began regaining strength gradually and one fine day as I was holding your right hand, I felt a little twitch, when I looked you were trying to squeeze my hand as we do ever so often. I was so happy I ran to tell your Doctor and he told me yes he observed that there are times when there is a slight movement on the right side of your body. I smiled with glee as although it was only a twitch, for me it was as if you had gotten up and walked around the entire room.

It was at this point your first physiotherapist came into play. She was a very cheerful and happy individual. Her very persona alone I could tell willed her patients to do well and strive to complete any set task as it relates to recovery. Day by day she would arrive and do her sessions with you and soon you were strong enough to sit upright in a chair. The first morning when I came and saw you sitting I was so happy to see you out of the bed. It didn't matter that they had to use something to keep you upright or that your right hand was propped up on a pillow to prevent it from falling, for me the mere fact you were sitting up meant you were getting better.

We then developed a routine, I would get to your bedside as early as possible and have devotion before your physiotherapist arrived. Which was our normal routine back in the day before we left for work. This was what we were doing one morning when to my amazement you began humming then singing a few words as I sang "Trust in the Lord with all Thine Heart". It was such a miracle that swept in as gentle and as cool as the crisp summer breeze. It was the most amazing thing I ever heard, tears fell from my eyes and I said thank you Lord the connection is still there. It had your nurses at their station outside your room in tears and it had everyone on the floor smile in amazement at how real and true our Heavenly Father is. After we had our devotion that morning I knew things would never be the same and better days were ahead as renewed hope and strength visited us in that hospital room and so it was that after devotion I carried on my daily task of sorting out your amenities meanwhile you did physiotherapy. This I opted to be absent from as I realized when I was around you, you would focus all your attention on me and not on whoever was attending to you. For this reason I began excusing myself when something had to be done as I wanted you to focus on what they were doing and make the most of every session.

As the days progressed I remember your physiotherapist was waiting on me one morning and she told me how heartbroken you were when you realized the walking motion was very challenging. Being the positive and energetic person she was, she began encouraging me and letting me know ways I could help with your recovery for example playing your favourite songs in the hospital room. This would help a great deal in the healing process by putting you into a better frame of mind. Her positive energy and attitude was one that I began to feed on daily. Each day I looked forward to speaking with her and getting an update on how you were. It didn't matter that when they lifted your hand or foot it fell back to the bed with a thud, it didn't matter that they had to feed you through a tube, or that almost everywhere there was a tube connecting you to a machine of some sort. As far as I was concerned you were alive and here was someone else along with your Doctor, nurses and myself, who saw that you were getting better and were giving advice on what I could do to help.

The day when you were finally able to go outside was one engraved in my heart forever. They had a special chair that had wheels on it, not like the typical wheelchair and looking back I think whoever designed it was very wise. It made one feel as if they were seated in a King's chair with a high back and arm rests, so although you were being pushed around one would not even realize that they were not in control of their own movements. As they opened the door to your balcony the glee in your eyes when you felt the fresh air against your cheeks was amazing. This was the first time in weeks you were being outdoor and the overall effect it had on you was amazing. As you rolled passed the janitor who was seated on the ledge on your left, you held out your hand to her and tried to nod in greeting. The same for the porters who assisted you to and from your chair, although you were unable to say thank you, you would do so with a slight nod. I smiled as who you were at heart began shining through as everyone you passed you attempted to greet and my heart rejoiced as this was what you would normally do.

When it came to warmth, smiles, genuineness and seeing the good in everyone that is you. I can truly say I am blessed with a husband whose love and care has no bounds. It doesn't matter who it is, where they are from or what they have done, from the day I met you I realized you extended warmth to all. It still amazes me at times as even the most difficult personalities that we have come across, within minutes you would have them smiling. There was even a time at your workplace where you got a prize for the one most likely to make others smile and this was so true. Not only would you make persons smile but in all the years I have been blessed to have you in my life I have never heard you make a negative utterance about anyone. In fact you taught me that everything in life is a choice, including choosing to see the positive in everyone, every situation and every circumstance. This day as you ventured outdoors I was reminded of it all as having being restricted to your room with only nurses, doctors and myself, being outside around others was an opportunity for you to socialize and extend your warmth to others as you would normally do.

Day by day I also developed a daily routine for myself; wake up, seek God's face, give thanks and get to your bedside as soon as possible. Not only did I miss your presence while I was away but one morning the nurse on duty told me that throughout the night you had difficulty sleeping as you kept looking for me as you awaited my return. I knew immediately in my heart what was wrong, usually when we part from each other's presence we would call each other to say we have arrived safely to our destination. In this case I would leave the hospital late at nights and you would have no idea if I got home or to my cousin's house ok. So I purposed in my heart that as much of the twenty four hours given in a day, a majority of it in fact as much as possible will be spent with you. With this being the case I had no desire to go to the canteen much less to stand in the line and purchase food and that was how my mom and your brother began bringing me food. I literally had no appetite and though my mom could not come inside the hospital room, she would wait patiently on the balcony for me to come out and have a bite. Your brother too would do the same, this he would do even when he took public transportation to the hospital in order to drive me home. This he did as we all knew that driving long distances was not recommended as my emotions were in turmoil. This I admired so much and I thought to myself if I had an older brother I would want him to have many of his character traits. The nurses too were very kind, usually they would find me asleep with my head on the rail of the bed or on the chair's armrest if you were seated in the chair. At times, they would leave an extra blanket out for me, suggest I sleep in another chair to ease the tension off my back or encourage me to have something to eat or drink. Although I was quite contented with just sitting and holding your hand, I knew deep down that they had my best interest at heart and that they were right.

With a majority of the days spent at your side, from then on I observed and learned what the various machines were, how to read them and what each tube meant, how to prop you up in the chair, to name a few. It was on one such day while you were in the chair, I sat facing you and fell asleep. When I woke up you were looking at my wedding ring and you were able to communicate to me that I should always wear it so that you would always remember. Tears filled my eyes and I showed you yours which I had on my right hand as from the day I took it off your finger when you were going into surgery, I told myself I would wear it for you until you were able to. At that point in time everything stood still and as I looked at you, I no longer saw all the wires and the tubes, I saw you and I thanked God for not only giving you to me but also for keeping you. I thanked Him for our marriage and most importantly for our love, a love that transcends all space and time.

Soon the day came when you would be given something to eat by mouth and I got to your room praying all would go well, as I know if it did that would be one less tube for you and if it didn't I didn't even want to think about what that meant. When I got there to God be the glory I was informed by the nurse that you had a strong appetite. You had all your breakfast and managed to keep everything down. I felt so good about that and I was mindful that God was on your side. I had our usual devotion and waited patiently for your Doctor to arrive as no matter how my day is going, speaking to him always reinforced the calmness that I willed myself to feel. Not only did I receive updates on how you were doing but I also look forward to his positivity and the wealth of knowledge he obtained. He was one who was very upbeat and cared deeply for his patients, I learned at an early stage of your recovery process to listen to what he had to say as not only did he possess a wealth of knowledge but he also shared his knowledge and gave solid advice to guide me through every step of the way.

# When you thought your world caved in…then the wind came & threatened what Remained

IT'S AMAZING how the mind thinks and how as humans we are able to compartmentalize things in our mind. Since the day you became ill, you were my sole focus. Nothing else mattered other than your recovery, seeing you and spending as much time as possible at your side. However deep down I knew it would only be a matter of time before I had to face the harsh reality that there were other things that I am going to have to deal with as time stops for no one.

The dreaded day finally came one day when I was seated on your balcony while the nurses made their rounds. After leaving you in their care I sat looking for the bird perched in its usual location when my phone rang, it was regarding one of the bills for your surgery. I was informed that I had to come in and make some arrangement to cover the cost and the total was over One Million Dollars (J$1,000,000). It wasn't their call that made me uneasy it was the fact that God had not yet given me the answer to my question regarding where the money would come from to settle the medical bills. I knew by standing on His word and my faith, that it would be paid. I just did not know when and where it would come from and that made me uneasy.

It just so happened that the call came in on the very same day I was told by your Doctor that I needed to mobilize some funds. This I could understand as he had already completed your surgery, a twelve hour brain surgery, without even a deposit; and I had assured him he would get his money. I knew better than to take any of the requests for payment personally as the reality is that many individuals in the world we live in today are not honest. The sad reality is that the culture that we live in is one where many are not trustworthy or genuine and this paints a very bad picture right across the board to include those who are honest. The truth is there have been cases of individuals foregoing payments of their medical bills, some do this by even migrating to other countries. However once again I assured him that I was putting things in place and that I am definitely working on it. To be honest I was, as I was looking at the options before me. Which would be to sell our home, car and everything in our possession;

then find a way to explain it to you afterwards as at no point could you know about the amounts outstanding. I had already made up my mind that if that was what it takes I was prepared to sell everything we own in order to keep you alive as we could always start life over together. I didn't have a choice really, as there was no way I could endure life without you. However even selling all that we owned would just be a drop in the bucket when it came to the total owing. Even then I made a vow to myself that you can never know about this as you would be consumed with concern and at no point should you be worried. I remember saying to God, "God I will only mention the amounts outstanding to Marvin only when the bill has been paid in full". It was a burden I decided to bear alone as there was no way you could undergo that stress and strain in the critical condition you were in. That very night when I got home I poured out my heart to God while giving Him thanks. You had recovered enough to say two words "yes" and "ok" and that was the only thing you would say. When asked if my name was "Sarah" as you were unable to say no you would just keep silent until they asked if this is your wife, then you would say "yes". You being able to say a few words and so soon was a blessing. I began giving thanks for your progress as although I was plagued with concerns ranging from the surgical fees to the mounting hospital bills and money required for your care, you were talking. Regardless if it was just two words you were able to speak them.

I began to see just how easy it is for one to lose focus and miss the blessings that lined each day. Here you were speaking and that in itself was so much to be thankful for. Yet if I was not careful it was so easy to be concerned about all that seemed to be going wrong and that would hinder me from seeing all that was going right, in this present moment. This would result in being blinded and refusing to give thanks for those prayers that were being answered as my focus would be on those prayers in my view that have not been answered as yet. It was then I realized a strategy that the enemy uses, that of mind control. If he can control your mind then he will hinder your praise and your "praise party" that is intended to last will be replaced with that of a "pity party". Now the difference is that a "praise party" abides in true worship and thanksgiving from your heart, setting the platform for miracles, signs and wonders from Almighty God. A "pity party" on the other hand renders you immobile, feeling sorry for yourself and focusing on all that seems to be going wrong. This cripples your faith and limits the move of

God's hand in your life.

Though I was already nervous about all that you were going through, after receiving that call regarding a bill with a total of over One Million Dollars, my thoughts were in shambles. However regardless of how I felt deep down I refused to stop my praise. I then realized that when you feel as if you are really at the bottom of an endless pit you can only look up and there you will find God; and upon finding Him you just have to praise Him for how awesome He really is. I warred that night in the spirit against principalities and powers that would hold up the source of these funds, harden the hearts of those whom we had to deal with, place discouragement in our minds, and prevent those in charge of your care not to treat you with divine favour. These things I know, if they prevailed, could prevent me from letting me take the path God has made for me and in turn for us as it would threaten my sanity and peace of mind. I prayed continually and fervently and that was how I fell asleep, leaving it all at Jesus's feet. Little did I know that the next phone call would tilt what's left of the foundation of what held my already fallen world together.

The following morning my mom called, she who has been one of my strong tower sounded a bit distant that morning. However I told myself it was the long haul of the past few day's events that were taking its toll. After checking up on me she hung up and immediately after my dad called. This time I knew something was definitely wrong. It turned out that my mom's dad, my grandfather had died earlier that morning. I was in total shock and I listened as if I was in a scene of a movie as dad told me what happened, how he fell ill, was rushed to the hospital and then slipped into another world. I thought to myself this was not happening, that this was all just a bad dream and certainly in a few minutes I would wake up and Marvin would be home getting ready for work making jokes and all while I prepare breakfast and that granddad was still in the country looking over at the hills and valleys from his chair on the verandah and talking about how lovely the scenery is. But the reality was he was gone and it hit me forcefully that I had to do all I can, by standing on faith I didn't even know I had, to prevent my husband from slipping through those very same doors into another world.

This turning point made me realize that man in himself is so limited. Limited by his very own limitations as there was nothing I could do, I had to turn to the creator himself our Heavenly Father for strength to make it through. I did not have the time to mourn or break down in tears as if I did I know that the composure I had to keep calm and deal with your situation would come crumbling down. I had to be strong especially for you as I had to fight for you as you were unable to fight for yourself. There was no way I could let you know granddad had passed as you both were always sitting and chatting away on each of our visits. He called you his "young lad" a name that always brought a smile to your face and I knew that you would have been deeply saddened by his passing. I thought of my grandmother many days as I sat by your bedside, I wanted so much to be there but I know you needed me more. I remember when I called her on one occasion and she said to me "look your grandfather is gone but your husband is here, stand by him and do what you have to do for him, as nothing we do can bring your grandfather back".

In my tribute to him at his funeral I mentioned the many summers my cousins and I spent in the country with my grandfather and grandmother as grandchildren. Summers filled with the laughter: of children ringing in the atmosphere, of happier days from going with him to tend to the goats, reap peanuts you name it. Looking back it's no wonder I ended up in finance at some point in my chosen career path as he used to rear and sell goats including those of my own and he was the first to put a large sum of money into my tiny little hands as a child from such a sale. Even now I remember him saying to me "always check monies given to you even if it is from grandpa then put it up safely in the bank". I also thought of his advice when I was getting married, how he told me "where I am bound that is where I must obey". I thought of his love and acceptance of you as my husband and how on our last visit three days before you fell ill we had such a great time laughing, talking and sharing as always. Never did we know that would be the last time we would see him. These were the thoughts that filled my mind as I sat at your bedside, wanting to pour my heart out to you, you my very best friend whom I could always share my innermost thoughts with. However as I held your hand and watched you sleep, I took heed to my grandmother's words. There was nothing I could do to bring grandpa back but I was even more determined that you had to survive as there was nothing more my heart could take. For this reason I decided to mourn granddad's passing after we got through this and along with the mounting bills I added one more thing I would withhold from you at least for now as there is no way I could tell you of his passing.

It's at this point in one's life you realize the importance of support systems. I always knew we were loved and each day I was reminded even more just how much. The love and support shown from our immediate family, church family, work family, friends and well-wishers was amazing. Whether it was a note, a card, gas money you name it persons thought of it and they ensured they did it with love. It reminded me that no matter what race, colour, religion or gender there is one thing that we all have in common and that is the fact that we are humans and we all have a heart and a sense of purpose that reflects God's goodness. He uses whom and whoever he chooses to bless us and looking back I am eternally grateful for all who were obedient to His voice. From the prayers to the gifts to the encouraging word or notes it was and still is greatly appreciated to this very day.

As the days went by the day finally came when follow up brain scans were to be done to see how things were post-surgery. As with so many times before I stood at your bedside explaining to you all that was about to happen. That an ambulance will be coming for you and that you will be doing another scan to ensure the surgery went well. It was at that point I saw you bow your head and tears filled my eyes as I knew exactly what you were doing as this was a usual routine for us before any major event or before any long journey. We would find each other, hold hands and bow our heads as we prayed. With emotions choking me I managed to whisper "are you praying?" And you nodded yes. When the ambulance came I watched as they placed you on the stretcher and I walked behind you down the corridor. Only your nurse on duty was allowed to go with you and once more I watched as they closed the doors of the ambulance, turned on the flashing lights and drove away. I couldn't help it, the tears rushed down my cheeks as I felt as if I was reliving this moment again. It was then I heard you brother say "no, no, no, everything will be ok". I don't even remember getting into the car or even him driving us to where the scans will be done. But I do remember sitting in the waiting room once more trying to remind myself that although fear is right beside faith and hope it doesn't mean I have to stop and entertain it. After what seemed like an eternity we were told that the procedure went well and we should await the results to take to the doctor.

After getting the results and settling the bill we took it back to the hospital and thanks be to God it showed that the surgery was a huge success and healing is taking place wonderfully. I was ecstatic, God came through again and all was going well on your path of recovery. As the days turned to weeks, the cell phone conversations regarding settling medical bills became more arduous and frequent. I fought to keep my emotions at bay, as I know you were always so in tune with my emotional state of mind and at no point could I let you know all that I was going through. I was at the place where I was seeking God for direction for the medical bills, your recovery and comfort for my family as we mourn the loss of a loved one - my grandfather. All three were enough to let me just want to hibernate for a while. But I know that would and could not be the case. Unlike the other times in the past when I sought God, this time I could not go into isolation or be by myself I had to find a way to do it while being there for you in every way I can.

When the day finally came when I was told that being home in your familiar surrounding would help you to heal faster I was so happy, I was over the moon. There were many clauses and conditions I had to adhere to including sourcing a special bed, following specific meal plans, fostering and maintaining a controlled environment, administering injections to name a few.

The latter of which I would be normally terrified of as I did not like needles. However on this occasion I decided I will just have to learn and interestingly I was happy to. So after being taken through and shown what will be required of me to care for you, I accepted. In fact I gladly accepted all the conditions as you were coming home and that was all that mattered. I can never forget the moment we got the go ahead and we could leave, I had already packed all your things in anticipation and as I assisted you from the bed I heard when it was decided that no wheelchair was to be requested and to be honest I was extremely grateful as I know that would have definitely cramped your spirits. So it was that in a matter of two weeks you were able to go home and unlike others who did similar procedures, you were able to walk out of that hospital even though it was with assistance. This was given by your brother on your right and your cousin on your left. Though it took some time to get the walking motion, you did and you made it. I watched in awe as you got in the car, looked at me, held my hand and smiled. We were going home.

It was at that point I realized what your Doctor meant when he said familiar surroundings will assist with the healing process as when we got to the stop light the first thing you did was put the safety locks on the car doors on. This had me smiling as this is what you would usually do. The journey home took forever well at least to me as I sat wondering if you were ok, if you would remember our home and how you would react to it all. When we drove up the driveway I heard your brother telling you this was your house and showing you all around. I saw my mom's jeep parked a few houses away and I knew she was doing the final preparations to our home for your arrival. I also wondered how she was doing today as the loss of her father was still very painful, yet she was here. I thank God for her and your brother every day as regardless of what they were going through, there was never a time I needed support they were not there.

# Chapter ix

# Living by God's leading…the journey continues at Home

THE FIRST thing you did when you were assisted into the house was sit in the armchair, then to my amazement you reached and attempted to turn on the television and pointed to the speakers for your brother to turn them on for you. I kept on saying thank you Jesus barely above a whisper as I could not express my gratitude enough. I felt as if my mind could not conceive the very words to thank God for all He has done and continued to do for us. I was already seeing evidence of what your Doctor said regarding coming home and being in your own environment being a definite plus as it speeds up the healing process with certain items bringing back a particular memory. Seeing you motioning for the television and speakers that you had connected, to be switched on brought such joy to my heart. After giving you your meal and staying by your side, I realized the medications were taking their effect and tiredness was settling in. We assisted you to the bed that was placed in the other room for you and

I saw you briefly glance around before lying down. This glance I knew was due to the fact that I had arranged with your niece and a friend of ours for the room to be decorated with simple artifacts that you loved. I wanted a calm and happy environment for you and tried my very best to create a space that not only provided this but one you would love as well.

It's interesting how watching someone perform a task made a task seem relatively manageable and often times easy. The reality however is totally different, as although I watched the nurses many times in getting you prepared and settled in for a night's rest, it took me close to an hour before I was satisfied that you were ok and I didn't hurt you in the process. I was however very thankful of the bond we share and that made it easier as with you responding  very well to my voice, I was able to coax you into shifting here and there in order to make the task at hand easier.  After getting you settled I kept checking if all was well as I feared you bumping your head on the rails of the bed. Eventually I felt better by wrapping the rails with a soft towel and then I sat down and found myself watching the rise and fall of your chest to assure myself you were breathing as in my mind there was nothing here to monitor your heartbeat.

This was how my mom found me hours after when she came to check in on me, just sitting on the edge of my makeshift bed beside yours watching your chest move to ensure that you were breathing. It was at that point I realized just how long I sat there and she reminded me that "God can do what I am unable to do" and she decided to stay with us that night. I knew what she meant as there is no way I would be able to keep my eyes on you twenty four hours a day or seven days a week but our Heavenly Father is equipped to do just that and more. To my delight you slept well that night as long as my hand remained clasped in yours through the rails of the bed. As I was much lower than you this proved a challenge for me but nothing would prevent me from enabling you to get a good night's rest, even if it meant sleeping in a cramped position. We had waited for this day for so long and your happiness and peace of mind was crucial to me, after all you were home.

Morning came and by the time you woke up, I was trying to visualize our day and your brother arrived just in time to help me figure it all out. While mom assisted me with your diet and specific meal preparations that were to be made daily, he assisted me in figuring out the physical aspect of your healing process. This we worked on regarding how to get the walking motion going daily by having an action plan for each morning and evening.  This we eventually did by balancing you and assisting you from the house to the gate, this was no easy feat by myself as not only were you weak but I was not tall enough to balance you effectively. While I could assist you to the chair and back, it took someone much stronger to venture with you outdoors. Pretty soon we had a little routine going on and each morning I would have devotion and have you up, dressed and ready for your brother's arrival; he would in turn take you for walks outdoors and back. This he managed to do before going to work even if it means getting to us extremely early when he had to go in on an early shift. There were even days when he would begin working and ask for permission to leave for just a few minutes to visit.  On other days he came early and after walking you he would hasten to catch a ride with a co-worker who was passing by. The same went for in the evening as he would come and do the same. There was never a time that we needed him that he was not there; in fact he came by every single day. For evening walks he ensured that we got everything done in time before I had to administer your medication. He never missed a day and he never missed an appointment in taking you to the physiotherapist which initially was a daily event as intense physiotherapy was recommended.

The first day we took you to see your physiotherapist we both had to assist you in walking from the car to the reception area. I was deeply concerned about your balancing as your coordination was a bit off and I remembered the physiotherapist at the hospital expressing her concern on the different areas of your body that needed to be addressed. I however pushed aside all fears and focused on speaking to my soul "he shall not die, I will not die, he will walk by himself again and if he is going through this then he was made for it and if we are going through this we were made to overcome it, as together we are stronger". I had previously learnt the art of speaking to my soul from my best friend. It's something she taught me during one of our many conversations when she was encouraging me on how to make it through this difficult phase. This art she developed over time when she was going through a rough time in which she had to remain strong for her father who was battling an illness. This helped a great deal as I realized that there are times when you have to speak life even into your very own situation as regardless of how dim it may seem, there is power in words.

Your second physiotherapist was a wonderful individual and even though getting you to perform certain tasks was a bit difficult she remained calm and encouraging, even when she had to improvise ways and means for you to perform these said tasks. It was in times like these we pulled strength from your brother's presence and it had a great impact on calming both our nerves. It was one morning after your brother arrived for your morning walk when he decided that we can extend your walk a bit by walking to the backyard and do the exercises given at physiotherapy. I know it was the best thing to do and that it was necessary, however I got scared that you would hurt yourself as you were barely walking. The niggling thought kept lurking around, what if he fell? What if his balance and coordination was not back as yet? It was at this point in my life I began seeking God in prayer asking Him not to let me hinder your progress due to my own fears and insecurities. I then changed the "what ifs" to that with a positive connotation, "what if this is what he needs to heal? What if this is what will boost his confidence of having a perfect gait and balance again?" These positive thoughts along with speaking to my soul calmed the raging storm within me and eventually the negative thoughts drifted away. The truth is there was so much happening around me that I had to tune everything else out except being positive and relying on my faith.

Apart from your recovery process which was paramount I was also dreading returning to work which I would have to do in the next two weeks. I dreaded it so much as I often wonder how on earth I would be able to go to work and leave you; since all this I have never left your side. I was also terrified of you hearing about the mounting medical bills among so many things. Your recovery and peace of mind were my constant aim. I prayed about it, fasted about it, lived for it and in turn thrived on your recovery, the better you did the better I felt. It was so much so that one day when my mom came to drop off the grocery bags, she saw me preparing dinner for you. She then asked me something that made me realize that I had totally forgotten about myself since our lives changed. She asked me, "So what are you having for dinner?" I then realized in planning and preparing your meals, scheduling and administering your medication among so many things, I literally forgot about myself. There was nothing left in the pot after I took out your dinner. For the first time in my life I cooked for one individual without even realizing it. She then sat me down and reminded me of the importance of taking care of myself. I was reminded that yes your recovery is mandatory but if anything happens to me it will impact you negatively. I was also reminded that if I became ill it would be total chaos as well as I am the only one that was allowed to be around you twenty four seven and the last thing you needed was to hear that I was not well. Needless to say I heeded to her words as I know deep down she was correct. No matter how hard it was to find a sense of peace in the chaos I still had to muster up enough peace of mind to care for myself too. Not only could I not afford to be ill I could not afford for you to be worried about me being ill either and for that reason I made a concerted effort.

It was on one of those evenings after we had dinner I sat wondering what my next step of action would be as God had been so good that my request for two weeks' vacation leave was granted so I was able to stay home and care for you. After the first week was finished I remember saying to my mom I really want you to be able to be walking by yourself even a bit before I headed back to work. As although a caregiver would be there I was not sure how you would react to that. Her reply was one I will always remember; she said to me "let us speak it into being". I smiled as I knew she was making reference to the scripture in the Job 22:28 which says as children of God we can decree a thing and watch it come to pass. There were many things to perplex my mind but I realized that once again it was up to me to choose which door I knocked on as before me there was the door of hope, fear, faith and anxiety.

Since your return home from the hospital I had more time with my thoughts and I was reminded of some of the harsh realities that I faced. I was a thirty one year old wife, caring and fighting for her husband's life. One whom after Insurance owed over Five Million Dollars (J$5,000,000) in surgical bills and was faced with rising rehabilitation fees for relevant therapies. All these I decided to keep to myself without your knowledge until when all outstanding medical fees were paid as I preferred to bear this burden though unbearable it may seem, rather than placing your life into even more jeopardy as worrying at this point was a no no for you. I told myself no matter how it seemed or felt I know that this was not the end and if I just kept putting one foot before the other I will get to another door that had faith and hope written on it.

It was after the first couple days of being home that I was about to get you settled for bed, that you shook your head saying no and pointed to your own bed in our master bedroom. I smiled and my heart melted as not only did you point to the bed you pointed to your side of the bed as well. I then assisted you up on the bed and somehow we managed to get you in the laying down position and the smile that was on your face was so worth it. In doing this though anxiety began creeping in my mind, which I had to put at bay. For example the thought of you bumping your head on the wall was enough to have me stay up all night watching you. I then asked God what to do and felt a sense of relief when I was led to line very soft towels at the side of the bed closest to the wall. Sleeping in your own bed became the order of the day and the more you relaxed and slept the more comfortable I was. We then developed another routine, and each night before going to bed you would beckon to me to pray and each morning when I awake we had prayer once more. Morning prayer usually included me anointing your body from the crown of your head to the soles of your feet as I knew that God could heal you totally giving you full restoration, one with perfect gait and balance, one who I knew God would elevate higher than ever before and turn what the enemy made for bad into good into our lives. As you loved hearing me sing I sang a lot too to keep you going, to keep myself going and to just change the atmosphere to one of thanksgiving and adoration in our home.

The time drew nigh for me to return to work as my four weeks off which included both compassionate and vacation leave came to an end. With this being the case, I began seeking God even more in my prayer time. It was my desire to have you balancing to a large extent on your own before I returned to work. Yes a caregiver would be with you during the days but just the thought of leaving you was unbearable. I remember each day as the time winded down saying to my mom once more how I felt regarding it all and she said just continue speaking it into being. I began doing that I began speaking it over your life, into our lives and into the very atmosphere. Here once more I was reminded of the power of words. As just before returning to work you did just that, yes you needed some assistance but day by day, especially with daily physiotherapy you were getting there.

# Chapter x

# Angels all around...

IT IS important to realize that as a child of God our very place of abode and in turn our address is not by chance. I believe it is something that God has fashioned from the foundation of the earth. When we moved into our home after we were married we did not foresee the future and what was in store. But as it is your physiotherapist who just so happened to be the best in this region of the island and head of the physiotherapist board had her practice just a two minutes' drive and a ten minute walk away. Where I was employed was also just an eight to ten minutes' drive away depending on the traffic and we were surrounded by a host of supporting neighbors and friends.

When the dreaded day came that I was to return to work I felt a wave of sheer panic wash over me. Since our lives had changed there was never a day when I was not at your side. I was feeling so down about it that I had to make a conscious effort to continuously give praise especially for the fact that you were recovering and rapidly too. After arranging for a caregiver to be present in my absence I ensured that she was present to understudy me before I returned to work in order to understand our routine. Once again I began speaking to my soul and reminding myself that God has everything under control. The first day for me was the hardest and it seemed as if the time for my lunch break would never arrive. This began another routine that day, which involved coming to see you each day in my lunch hour. It was during one of these visits as we were sitting outside as we normally do when you asked if I had lunch as yet. I smiled as I knew what you meant and what you were asking, the truth was lunch was the farthest thing from my mind, all I wanted to do was to see you and spend time with you during the allotted hour. In the end I said "no" and you gave me the look that meant please ensure you do. It was at that time my mind took me back to one of my hospital visits when your Doctor reminded me that I had to keep it together in order to ensure that you did not begin to worry about how I was coping. Hence I assured you that I would and headed back to work.

God was so good to me that when I resumed work the pile I expected to be sitting on my desk, was nowhere to be seen. Even my workload God took into consideration and my co-worker whom I worked closely with managed to man my desk as best as he could in my absence even though we were already short staffed. The tears that flooded my eyes was one of gratitude to Almighty God as He thought of everything at every stage of our journey. The outpour of love and well wishes from my work colleagues was amazing. Even those who I did not work closely with were sending up prayers, fasting and sending in various prayer requests at churches both locally and overseas for us. With all the love and support that surrounded us I saw God's hand everywhere. When you had gained enough strength for us to go for early morning walks I watched in amazement at how persons in close proximity to us chipped in. Initially it was just us and day by day as you got stronger and stronger others who knew they could help wanted to help and did so.

Soon one of our neighbour and our friend began doing exercise sessions with you. As he was trained in this area he focused on strength building which included strengthening your muscles along with working on your balance and coordination. He was so dedicated that he did this every single morning and for those mornings when he worked out of parish he would inform us beforehand. As time went by, walks and workouts became a normal routine and if he was unable to schedule workouts his son would chip in and carry on. One morning when they were unavailable we went for a short walk and you decided that you wanted to do another block by yourself, once more I became unsettled. I knew that it was inevitable that the day would come when you would want to regain your independence and with this in mind I said ok. Immediately as you continued, without even thinking I began speaking to my soul and it immediately calmed me. As I too continued my walk and I deliberately waited at the end of each block where I could see you, to appease myself that you were alright.

I learnt that day that there are angels all around us and we have to pray and trust them to do their work (Psalm 91:11-12). Each of us have been assigned an angel at birth and if we think about it there are millions of angels all around. On that morning while speaking to my soul I reminded myself that there was an angel watching over you and nothing would harm you. It wasn't that I doubted you would be fine but I remembered once we were walking and some thorns that were in the pathway grabbed your hand. I remember pondering what to do then and fortunately we were near our Bishop's house and his wife who happens to be a nurse took a look at it and sent us off feeling so much better. Eventually I learnt that it's not possible to see and protect one from everything. There comes a time when we just have to let go and let God do what He is equipped to do. Pretty soon we adjusted our routine to include our morning walks and it was at this aspect of your recovery I realized just how crucial time really is. In the midst of all that was happening it was continuously reinforced that it is of key importance. It wasn't that we did not value time, it was just that during the recovery process I imagine a sense of emptiness settled in and there was always the fear that one wasn't doing what they should. After seeing this was the case as you feared time was passing you by, to eliminate your fears of uncertainty, I created our very own timetable at home. This worked remarkably well as this I placed at strategic points in our home. I ensured to include from devotions, early morning walks we took together, things to do in the days and the time when I would return home from work. This I incorporated with my personal schedule to ensure that my time coincided with yours. I realized that for those who choose this route making breakfast and dinner preparations for the following day does wonders in creating a balance.

As the days went by I was torn between being elated and excited at how well you were doing as soon you were asking for family members including your niece and nephew whose mother, your sister had recently passed. This you did by taking up their pictures and asking me if they were okay. My heart melted as you loved your departed sister dearly and the well-being of her children meant a great deal to you. That same night you asked me about the house and other monthly payments that you would normally make by showing me the bills. This I reassured you was fine. Soon after you were asking for one of your closest friend whom you went to high school with and who was more like a brother to you. This you did by writing his name and I remembered the day your sister-in-law asked me who this person was. All these things made me extremely happy and your calm loving personality was still intact as I saw aspects of such, each and every day. So much so that one morning you reminded me that it was your caregiver's birthday and if I could arrive home early from work so she could have an early evening off to celebrate. I saw all this and the happier you did the happier I was, but in the back of my mind I kept thinking about your medical bills. Once again I made up my mind to be happy and to remain positive as being anxious and worried only made things worse. This I knew because if I did that the more agitated and absent minded I would be and you needed my full support in recovering.

Having a positive mindset enabled me to be grateful each and every day for the angels around us that I believe brought peace in turbulent times. As your healing process continued on a miraculous path we were however, not immune to a few hiccups on the road of recovery. The human body is an intrinsic and fascinating workmanship of the creator and each and everything is interconnected in a unique way. With this being the case recovery came with balancing and coordination, double vision among other things as your brain healed. Things relatively new to us but not to your Doctor and with him, the constant prayers being sent up along with God's guidance, we were able to overcome these challenges. He reinforced how critical your health was and stressed the importance of us adhering to his advice given from his expertise and knowledge. It's key to note that not every advice given was met with a favorable response, but for fear of your very life I made a vow in my heart to do the best I could with God's leading. Soon walking and holding your hand in order for you to balance, eye patches and panic attacks were hurdles that we were able to overcome one by one. These things I rejoiced and remained focused on as day by day you were doing better.

# Trusting & understanding God…in the cold, dark, Abyss

WITH YOUR Doctor's check up being initially every two weeks, I found myself at my wits end each time we were to go for your review. It wasn't that I doubted how well you were doing, as I know God was working a miracle in you and through you. But I was at my wits end as for six months post-surgery I still did not have the money to pay for the remainder of your medical bills. My mind was in constant turmoil over what to say to your Doctor as each visit approached. I had initially decided I would pay something on the bill no matter how small it was, while I waited for God to come through. This I did as soon as I got paid each month, however as the months went by I was beginning to wonder if this was enough. It was at this point I realized how lonely carrying a burden by yourself for a long time can become. I felt as if I was on a journey and at this very moment I was in an abyss; a deep, dark, cold and lonely place. It was a place where not many ventured for fear of losing oneself and one's mind. For those who offered sympathy it was evident by words some used that they did not understand and to be honest it would be unfair of me to expect them to understand. With this being the case many did not know what to say, some mumbled a few words, some kept their distance while others offered empathy from afar. Yet each day I decided I must continue on this journey as one day I will reach the finish line and all will be well again.

I knew to many it seemed as if the odds were stacked high against me. A young woman who decided to sign her life over to the debtors for a balance of payment amounting to over Five Million Dollars (J$5,000,000). This she did in order to save her husband's life seemed so unreal. Moreover it was a decision she took with no regrets as she preferred to start life all over with him than to continue life without him. Many could never and will never understand the concept much more the situation. Some even advised me to forget about the stress and strain, forget about the bills and live life, as you were recovering. But l know in my heart of hearts that God would come through for us and I stood on His word and His promises in St. Matthew 21 vs 22 that anything we ask in faith believing we shall receive.

Pretty soon however my days became such that I

dreaded hearing my phone ring or messages coming in as with each ring or beep my heart skipped a beat. As the days turned into weeks and the weeks into months the more adamant the collectors became and each day I made it a point of duty to transform myself on the drive home daily after work. This I had to do as at no point could you see me stressed or worried for fear that you would realize that there was much more going on that met the eye. It was so much so that the night before one of your checkups I decided to literally fight this battle on my knees. I began praying for the atmosphere in the Doctor's office, to the words I would say to ask for some more time and although I had no idea how long I was bargaining for I trusted God to work out the rest. The next day after your checkup he asked to speak to me in private, this was our usual custom as you would wait for me in the waiting area with your brother who was always present. It was things like these that made me admire your Doctor even more. He had every right to demand his money, yet he more than anyone else, was cognizant of the fact that you should not be worried about anything at all especially an outstanding bill of such magnitude.

This day like so many others he inquired about his payment and about those who were working on assisting me with the bills, to which I asked for more time. In this visit I told him upfront I thought of my options, of selling our car and home but I needed both for your recovery process. The car to take you for checkups, to and from the relevant therapies and the house aids in your recovery as you gradually adjust to your usual routine. I knew this time my words had an impact as I believed that was when he realized that with all my heart I wanted to settle all outstanding amounts. With that visit being less strenuous than those before I realized something that I knew all along but had never really put in practice. Fighting a battle on your knees in the spiritual realm has remarkable results. I then decided to put this strategy in practice even more as I needed solutions and fast. Everywhere I turned things were happening in an attempt for me to question God, but I refused to do so. One of the things I did not want to hear was that there was the need for additional therapy and upon hearing that as we left his office, I wondered how you would pull through doing so many things at once. But once more God proved Himself strong as He said His strength is made perfect when we are weak as written in 2 Corinthians 12 vs 9. Hence after combing the island far and wide for a reputable speech therapist that was on the list that your Doctor recommended, we began these sessions. As speech pathologists are relatively uncommon in our country we had to go to another parish for these sessions and once more my mother came to my rescue as she decided to dedicate herself to transport you on these specific days for speech therapy. This new phase of recovery brought with it many different areas that we had to adjust to. Firstly it shifted our schedule as not only was it a difficult process, we also had to do speech orals at home every day of the week. It was also at this time I began including our five minutes heart to heart talks. Whereas words were a bit difficult initially, I was able to understand certain cues and clues that you used. This was a wonder to many, but to me it was just another blessing from our Heavenly Father as Love knows no specific language. As this aspect of recovery proved difficult for you, I began seeking God even more on your behalf and even in cases where I read scriptures for myself and sang songs for myself I did them a second time for you and I told God it was just until you are able to do these things for yourself. It was during this lengthened process of seeking God that the bible scripture when Elijah the prophet prayed for it to rain upon the earth began to have an entirely different meaning to me.

This bible scripture found in 1 Kings 18 had three specific elements that spoke to me. The first was that in verse 41 Elijah said to Ahab that there will be an abundance of rain, he did not say to Ahab that there "may be" an abundance of rain he said there "will be". This showed me that Elijah knew what was expected, what he wanted, and he knew the God he served and that it would come to pass. The second thing to note was that immediately after making this positive statement in the affirmative, he changed his entire position including his posture and went into prayer with expectation. Now the bible has it recorded that after he prayed he asked his servant to look toward the sea to see if the rain clouds were there and if the rain was coming. This he did for seven times after getting a negative response each time his servant looked and there was no sign of a change. This showed his persistence in prayer and his faith in God that it was only for a matter of time but what he is praying for will surely come to pass and the rain will come. The third thing to note was that Elijah knew the importance of a shift in the natural which reflected a mighty move of God and after the seventh time when his servant replied that he saw a little cloud rising out of the sea the size of a man's hand Elijah told him to begin making preparations for the rain.  The fourth thing to note is that while preparations were being made based on the "cloud as small as a man's hand", nature took its course and had to obey as the heavens became black with clouds and wind and there was great rain. Above all what I learnt the most was that when God told Elijah in verse 1 that it was going to rain upon the earth that was it. God knew Elijah had what it would take to make it rain as He had equipped him with power to do great and mighty things.

Having used Elijah's experience to fuel my drive for seeking God and obtaining the answers I needed from Him, for myself and in turn for us, I began growing in my Christian walk in a time when I felt like I was barely coping. It was here I was reminded that no matter how alone you may feel when you are going through, you are never really alone as God is always with you. The feeling of loneliness will sweep over you as you begin changing things around you by eliminating all the negative elements from your life. This change is necessary as you hone in on God and shut out everything else that's going on around you; even the turmoil within, as you focus on God, the only one that really matters. This is usually the time when God reveals Himself to us when we are going through the unknown and the only thing we can do is reach and hold on to Him. While waiting on God it is usually a time of self-introspection to ensure that if there is any delay to the answers you are not to be blamed. For me that meant ensuring that while in solitude, I dealt with matters of the heart that needed fixing. These included asking God to search my heart and remove any isms and schisms that have been abiding there over the years. Things that I may have left behind thinking they were okay, but things that God needed to deal with on a timely basis. So it was that day by day while seeking God I learnt that there are many aspects of our Heavenly Father that can be revealed to us.

It was during these times that I spent in His presence, I was directed on letters to write to various entities, how to write them and who to call regarding assistance with your medical bills. I realized that God speaks to us especially in times of deep distress; however we have to place ourselves at strategic points to hear His voice. Each of these letters I prayed and fasted about and out of those that I did, only three I was given the permission by the Holy Spirit to send off. Now it is vital when listening to the voice of God to understand that there will be many strategies the enemy will use to try and let you second guess your decision. This happened in an instance when I was being asked by many individuals around me why I did not send off a particular letter. As I listened to the outside forces I soon became agitated and confused. Once more I felt as if the world was closing in and I found a quiet place to pray. After kneeling on the said letter I felt at peace coming out of prayer that I should not send it. I then forgot about it and the waiting game begun as it related to a response from the other three letters.

It is also key to note that at times while waiting, what may seem like the answer may be a distraction in disguise. This happened a few months after I sent the letters. I received a letter in the mail that told me I qualified for a loan worth three quarters of the current amount outstanding. Not only was the letter addressed to me, it was also sent from one of the institutions I wrote to and was signed by the person I knew was in charge. I remembered thinking with tears in my eyes, was this the decision they made? and was this what they came up with in response to my letter? I read the letter over and over and sadly said to myself probably this was the answer I was waiting on. I then decided that night to take it to God in prayer and not to let my emotions take charge and get the better of me as they had to be under subjection to the Holy Spirit. That night I prayed and I reminded God that a loan would in no way help me now. I needed serious help and I needed someone to step in and cover these outstanding bills. An interesting clause to the letter was that it had a date on which the offer would no longer be valid and as the days went by I kept reminding myself this is not the answer.  It may look like it, sound like it and in dollar amount equates to a portion of it, but it was not the answer from Almighty God as I had asked Him to pay this one for me. When the date had arrived for the offer to expire I received another letter that the offer had now been extended. This was enough to make me second guess what I was doing and if I was on the right path, but I refused to be denied as I knew the God whom I served and He had never failed me yet.

# Chapter XII

# The Key to waiting with Endurance…

AS THE days turned into weeks and the weeks turned into months, the loan offer expired and everyone was upon me for their funds. I was even told at one point that if I did not make payment soon I would be hearing from their office. The responses were weak, the follow ups were dim and the outlook from the natural eyes looked hopeless. Of the three letters sent out, one was unable to assist based on their policy, the other who I was really counting on began giving me different alternatives which were not very helpful at all and only the last one which was the smallest of the three remained positive.

The interesting thing however was that a few days after the loan offer had expired I found out that it was a promotion that they were having and that letters were sent out to all their customers. It was not a decision made solely for me regarding my situation and in response to my letter initially sent, but one that was made in general. I am so grateful to God that He taught me how to put my emotions under subjection as I would have made a costly and very bad decision. As time went by I realized that keeping my eyes fixed on God was the only way I would make it through. Yes I was in a straight place and many wanted to help by giving advice but there is one thing I knew about individuals and it was that many had great ideas but none had a solution. Especially in cases like these all advice received had to be weighed as not all advice given is good or Godly advice. So it was one day after a long duration of writing letters, making phone calls, negotiating, bargaining and warring in the spirit that God showed me not to underestimate the power of small beginnings and His timing is perfect. Although I heard this and I knew God was coming through one particular afternoon after dropping you to the physiotherapist I headed back home and sat in the driveway in total despair. What was I to do? Just as that thought came to mind my phone rang and it was a church sister checking up on me. I told her how I felt and in encouraging me she reminded me of something really profound. She reminded me that God could have come through and sent assistance for the medical bills in a minute, hour or day and the fact that he has not done so as yet means that he is working on something big and I just have to continue waiting and trusting him.

Her reminder was just in time and it encouraged me to change my outlook on the waiting process as God had a bigger and better plan in store.

As I had perfected the art of transforming my thinking process while I awaited God's miraculous breakthrough with our finances and your continued recovery. I decided to focus on all the positives that surrounded me and in turn us. Apart from you becoming visibly better in each and every way, the overflow of love gifts also kept coming in each and every day. No matter how small it was someone thought of it all and I realized that although deep down I felt alone facing this battle the truth that I was not alone was reinforced by every thoughtful gesture. Although it is hard at times to remain positive and upbeat when on the inside there is total chaos, each and every day I am happy that the Holy Spirit resides on the inside of us, giving us power for service, speaking to and calming our fears. It was while waiting for a positive response, and longing for my mind to be at ease that I realized that even during the wait, life continues. In fact it continues with its many challenges and we have to continue day by day while fighting to survive. This was evident when I realized that the car papers were due to be renewed and I had no idea which agency you used or where you were in the process. Not only were the bills due, they were due and I had no clue what to do as in our marriage we had worked into a routine where you dealt with certain things and it was working perfectly well for us over the few years. ...or so we thought. However all is well when things are going well, but it takes one shift to throw off the entire equilibrium.

My fears heightened when I realized I did not have a contact person to renew the cover note, did not know which one of the agencies were handling it and did not know which one of our accounts our bills were paid from and on top of that which was the worst of all, I did not have a clue on where to begin finding out. The utility bills were not only in your name, they were also sent via email to your email address so the hopes of finding the account numbers from a paper bill was futile. All these facts before now I did not have a problem with as not only were you up to date with the latest in technology and electronic banking and statements which allowed you to do everything online. You were also a wonderful provider and protector and each month I didn't have to worry about bills, mortgages, or car payments. So much so that I could not even remember the last time I saw a bill around the house. It was just what worked for us, you dealt with the bills and I focused on grocery bills and other household things. Now however this had changed and in a way that was extremely frightening.

There was so much going on, so much I could not tell you, I wanted so badly to confide in you, my other half, my advisor, counselor and best friend. You always knew what to do, always had a deeper insight and was good at giving good Godly advice. However I was scared for your life, terrified I would be taken to court for your bills and on top of it all on edge with all the bills that were currently due. As I began walking around with my emotions on edge I decided I needed to do another fast as fasting combined with prayer changes the most difficult situations to that of a better one. It wasn't that I had not fasted before but this time I decided that my petitions regarding your bills needed to be heard and I decided that no matter what I still had to maintain my composure and trust God during the wait. The thing with fasting is that it cuts and clears the channels for effective communication with Almighty God and I decided that I would do an Esther fast as I needed my petitions to be heard and fast. The Esther fast is one that resembles that of a fast Queen Esther did in the bible in the book of Esther. Here she sought

God regarding voicing her petition to save her people and herself. This she did by proclaiming a three day fast among her people abstaining from food and drink. Now fasting in itself takes commitment and dedication, this in itself is not an easy feat and as it was I was at work and faced with so many challenges. Yet I know I had to do this. I had to gain strength to fight even more for my petition regarding assistance regarding your medical fees and I also needed strength to fight on your behalf in the spiritual realm regarding your swift and smooth recovery.

I know this fast was something I had to do and it was the very first time I was led to do this particular one. I knew it was worth the sacrifice as anything getting you and in turn us over this hurdle in our life was worth it. I literally felt like not only had my world caved in, but it caved in taking all my hopes and dreams with it. I was at the place where I was fighting to remain focused on the sky where I believed one day the sun would shine again. It was hard, it was extremely hard and I knew I had to remain strong for you regardless of all we were faced with. I was torn between my concern for you, mounting bills, medical fees and work each day. I prayed that life would return to some sense of normalcy and fast. I was in it for the long haul and committed to do something different instead of my usual chain fast or one from sunrise to sunset with the hopes of gaining different yet positive results. Little did I know that the waiting period that I was going through along with the earnest desire in doing this fast was geared to taking me higher in my Christian faith with Almighty God.

Thus it was I went on the Esther fast the third month since our life changed. Although I was at work I managed to seek God even more and delved deeper and deeper each day in His word. It was not easy but the driving force within for a change was enough to keep me focused. I will never forget the day I broke this fast, I headed home as always in a rush to see you and I found my mom, your brother and sister-in-law at our house. I know this was God's doing as it was the perfect setting for prayer. This we proceeded to do by forming a circle and have you seated in the centre. I prayed, we all prayed and you were nodding in agreement until to our amazement you began praying and this time you were speaking in another language and my heart rejoiced as you were speaking in your heavenly language, in the tongues of the angels and there was no speech impediment at all. After we finished praying I remained on my knees before

Almighty God, His presence was so tangible in the room and all I could do was just worship Him for all He has brought us through, all He has done and all He continued to do. I began thanking Him for all I had asked Him for and I worshipped Him as if it was already done. After I was finished your sister-in-law who is a Deaconess in our church asked me if I listened to you and realized what had just happened and I smiled and answered yes.

It was no wonder you were in agreement with our prayer as you love God with all your heart. In our morning devotions I always marvel when I overheard your prayers as they always involved going to the house of the Lord. To just wake up get ready and go to God's house. Day by day as your prayers intensified and one day it seemed as if you read my thoughts and asked me if we could just go by our church for a visit. Therefore I made a request one evening for the church keys to facilitate your request and take you inside the sanctuary. The entire experience was amazing to say the least. You walked down the aisle, looked at the benches and sat in your usual seat. I took my seat on the choir, the Choir Director took up his position as he, his wife and your sister-in-law accompanied us. While there we sang a song for you while the Choir Director directed our choir of three. The entire experience was breathtaking and I was totally in tune as I was just a few days out of the Esther fast totally renewed and refreshed. Before we left, you were asked your prayer request and your response made us all teary eyed. Your request was that you would get better soon to be able to come back to this house of worship. Again we prayed for you while placing you in a circle and for the second time while agreeing to the prayers offered up for you, you began speaking in an unknown tongue. We were all happy that evening as without a doubt we knew that God showed up as His presence was felt by everyone and He was indeed working in your life.

128

# Chapter xiii

# The Wait…

IT WAS evident God was at work especially in our lives and I took comfort in that and decided to remain as close to Him as possible during the wait. With this being my mindset I realized that as I waited in one of my darkest season of my life that in every situation whether great or small, God was right there. His awesomeness unfolded each and every day. As I sat reflecting on the different ways He was working in, the first thing I remembered was when I had to find out and settle a payment regarding our house. With you falling ill at the end of the month I was not sure if a payment was made and to make matters worse, if not I did not have the account number. I sat outside your hospital room wondering what to do, when a cousin of ours stopped by. This he did almost every day although he knew he would be unable to see you, but came by to give support. It so happened that on this particular evening while we sat talking I so happened to look at his Identification Card and glory be to God he worked at the same organization that I needed to make contact with and was able to assist me in acquiring all the information I needed.

A similar situation was that surrounding the car documents and information that I knew would be on your mobile phone. My only concern was if I would be able to figure out the password during the allotted trials given.  After trying to find all the information I needed to no avail I decided that I would have to try your phone and so it was one night I tried swiping all your fingers to unlock it, when I saw that that was not working I said ok I will try the backup password. I tried every combination I could think of and my heart began racing when I had only one chance left to get it right unless the entire phone would shut down completely. I began asking God to tell me what it was as accessing your emails via your phone was my last option. God smiled on me once more that day and my last attempt worked, you had used a combination of my bio data and I am eternally grateful to God for revealing it to me. Once more I saw God's hand working in our lives as I was able to get the information needed, contacted the company and sorted out the documents for the car. Another instance was when it came to accessing funds from our other accounts. Here God led my steps and enabled me to find my way on the path He made, bringing to my memory old passwords and information that we had shared many years ago. To Him be all honour, glory and praise.

Staying close to God also enabled me to be wise in certain capacities as the Holy Spirit began showing me things I had never seen before. One such thing is that at no point should I underestimate the enemy and his crafty devices as no matter how low you are he will kick you where it hurts the most. So it was that one day you asked me to take you to see your favourite football team in The Premiere League, I did not hesitate as I know how much you loved football. It was a wonderful match and we both enjoyed ourselves and persons who were acquainted with us were really happy to see you. It was after we were leaving however that I was reminded that many individuals still refuse to think before they speak and the enemy without hesitation will try to use such a person. As we were exiting someone approached you and began asking about your medical bills, the said bills that I was determined not to let you find out about before they were paid. Fortunately I was there and was able to interject before this information was disclosed, but the encounter was one that remained with me and reminded me that time was of essence as the longer it took for the fees to be settled the greater the chance of you finding out. I also realized that no matter how things seem to be spiralling out of control, there is at least one blessing in each day that we have to be thankful for. Even if we have to search for it and hold onto it for dear life. As it was, although we had that encounter where the bill amounts were almost disclosed, the day overall was terrific, the stands, players, cheers and entire atmosphere brought so much joy to your heart and in turn gratitude to mine. Here you were in your setting, doing your thing just as old times and I made a mental note and captured that moment in time.

It was important not to trivialize regular routines especially those that bring much joy as it brings with it peace of mind; setting the ground for a positive recovery. It was of key importance to also realize that at each stage of recovery there were certain phases. The phase immediately after surgery was the question of what's next?, the second phase was the overall concern regarding time as it feels as if time was passing by and life was at a standstill, the third was that of anxiety as where the healing process is going well, here came the ability to realize and take into account all that one is able and unable to do. The fourth phase was that of trying to feel a sense of worth and wellbeing as with all the changes taking place one will more than likely feel outside of their element. The fifth phase was that of attempting to prove to oneself that they are able to accomplish any set task and this helps in the process of recovery as challenges are embraced in areas one would not necessarily venture. It is important to note however that each individual's journey on the path of recovery is different but one thing that cannot be overemphasized is love. With love there comes patience, consistent encouragement, motivation and support. Love in itself creates and sets the atmosphere for hope to blossom and faith to endure. It is in these trials that positive reinforcements and assurance are needed daily. Especially where there are tasks or assignments to be done as a part of the recovery process. These tasks should be readily available and creative ways found in doing them.

Your recovery as the days went by continued to be nothing short of a miracle, it was as if God chose you specifically for a deeper realm of His miracle working power. Day by day there was marked improvement and day by day I prayed that soon the help with our finances as it relates to your medical bills would be answered. It is of my firm belief that when the battle intensifies in the spiritual realm and the victory is near that the path of a believer may get uncomfortable. Uncomfortable because the enemy will try to use various distractions to let you lose or shift your focus. So it was one day while checking our bank account online, as in a measure of faith from time to time I checked to see if any funds were deposited. I also ensured I had an account number on hand at all times as well, just in case I was called off guard and our account number was requested for a deposit. This particular day I went online, checked the account to see if there were any deposits then decided to pay a utility bill and between, the numerous messages and calls coming in regarding your bills, therapies you name it I accidentally selected the wrong currency to pay the bill. Not only was the amount in another currency it was also from an account that I was only on but I was not the primary holder. After getting the reference number I sat there just staring at the computer screen as I could not believe what just happened. I was already in over my head and now I had to find a way to rectify yet another situation.

The first thing I did was call the bank that the account was currently being held at, at this point they too were surprised that the transaction went through considering the currency and amount. I was then told that I had to contact the utility company and take it from there and that was when the drama began. It turned out that it would take a few weeks before the funds could be returned. So it was, I began writing letters, sending emails and going to the utility office to get a refund on top of all that I was already going through. I never knew I could endure so much pressure all at once, but then again I have never been at the place in my life where I literally understood that the steady outpour of love from our Lord never falters and that His unconditional love would never come to an end. I remember praying and asking God for a break just a time to regroup and focus solely on my husband, his recovery and how good God has been to me. I wanted to just sit and reflect in awe at God's love for me and His mercy as King David mentioned in Psalm 57 vs 10 that reaches to the heavens.

A few days later as I was reflecting on my next move in terms of how to explain to my family member the "accidental withdrawal of funds", I mean how does one explain a withdrawal that equates to over One Hundred Thousand (J$100,000)? Along with that I was also thinking of how to get you to spend a few days by the seaside as recommended by your Doctor. This I was told would help you by far and as you always loved the sea I had no doubts it would be a welcomed experience.

Upon hearing that, I also thought to myself, some time away with you in order for you to recuperate would be perfect; but the reality is that was in no way possible unless by some form of a miracle. While contemplating everything and trying to find even more solutions, I received a very interesting email. It came from a dear friend of mine living overseas and she wanted to know if it was possible for me to get a few days off from work in a few months' time. My initial response was that I could speak to my Manager and see, but deep down I was not too sure if such a request would be granted. Little did I know of the blessing that was in store. When the topic arose again this time she was adamant for an answer and after checking with my Manager to my amazement and delight I was able to say yes! Miraculously my request was granted that if I needed a few days off I would be able to get it. That was when I was informed that both her and her husband were booking their holiday and they chose Jamaica as their destination island to give us their support. There was even more as they decided to have us join them on their vacation here by booking us a room into their all expenses paid Beachfront Condominium. I remembered saying to myself that a few days by the seaside could only be made possible by some form of a miracle and a miracle it was. At this point in my life this would have been in no way possible as everything around me was depleted and more than anything I wanted a breath of fresh air to just recuperate then resume fighting these battles. This break was what we both needed and I was ecstatic, elated you name it and constantly moved to tears each time I thought about it. Never in my life had I experienced such an outpour of generosity and love altogether combined. God knew I was at breaking point and specifically moved in a way that I had not expected or even seen possible and I am forever grateful to them and thankful to Him.

With a few months left before we headed to the north coast to meet my friends, I began thinking of this much needed getaway quite often. I had to, and each time I did it always brought a smile to my face and warmth to my heart. This expectation was coupled with happiness as although the waiting process was tedious your recovery continued to amaze those around you. Things like regular household chores, checking up on due dates and appointments just few months after surgery was simply amazing. As the months went by and life in itself remained hectic I still believed with all my heart that we could and we would definitely make it. I woke each day believing I was one day closer in receiving assistance toward those outstanding bills and began picturing our lives returning to some sense of normalcy. I really believed that God would turn all things around for our good and all that He has brought and kept us through will be for His glory. This fact was reinforced a few months after surgery when a close friend of ours came by for a visit. He had been ill at some point in his life and from what he recalled of his illness, he did not know what to expect when he came to visit as he knew your condition was much worse. As it was when he arrived at our house that Sunday morning he had no idea what to expect.

His visit was one that left an indelible mark on our lives, he began expressing the joy he felt in seeing how well you were doing and used his past experience to encourage you about the future. Before I knew it you both were speaking about plans you both made years before and soon I realized I was not needed to assist with the conversation. What stood out most about that visit was that he told us that you always spoke to him about giving his life to Christ and he has always delayed. However he said once he saw you walking to the gate to open it and greeted him, he knew it had to be God. Not only were you walking at just a few months after being rendered paralyzed and unconscious, you remembered who he was and the historical facts and events that made you both friends. With that being the case he told us that he will delay no more and made a conscious decision right then and there in our living room to change his life, get baptized and go into his church. It was such an emotional moment for me and we watched with great pleasure as his life took on a different meaning with God at the forefront from that day onwards. That night I gave thanks for him and his family as I was reminded that regardless of who you are God will go to the utmost highest to bring you into His Kingdom and this is as a result for His love for us. A love that reaches to the heavens spanning the entire earth and so it was I said to myself here goes one soul for my Father's Kingdom. This meant that all we have been going through was not in vain. It was and still is my firm belief that since the day our lives changed the process we were going through, could not be without something good coming out of it. The same thing went for a few of our close friends, one told us that her mother started praying and returned to church as she sought God in prayer continuously for your healing. The Youths at our local church were ones who touched my heart immensely, they cried out to God like never before and continuously sought Him in prayer on your behalf.  It is amazing at how God can use something so bad and turn it around for a whole lot of good and it reinforced the fact that in each and every day in every situation of our lives there is a blessing and sometimes a miracle in store, we just have to be patient and look keenly to find it.

# Chapter xiv

# Beyond the Wait...

AS IT was, at six months post-surgery my phone had to be kept constantly on vibrate both at work and at home because now the calls and messages were continuous. I had not gotten the funds to replace what had been accidentally paid out of the US$ account, neither had I gotten any assistance with the medical fees that were outstanding. Life as it was, continued with my full time job, continuous physiotherapy, speech therapy, speech orals, constant reassurance and oftentimes other follow up examinations and tests that at times left us on edge. It was not that I dreaded the results as I knew with time you would be fine. However, I was more concerned about the level of frustration I imagined you were feeling on the inside. Along with all that I was also terrified that any day now someone would reveal the state of our finances to you.

It was in times like these that I was happy I began our Sunday morning routine of going out for breakfast, this we did once a month usually near pay day at a nearby restaurant. It was something we both looked forward to and not only did the restaurant have a nice setting, it also carried a fairly decent crowd and that meant from time to time we would run into one or two persons we knew. Little outings like these kept me grounded as the days turned into weeks and the weeks turned into months.  Each time I paused to think about it, I felt as if a noose was being tightened around my neck each day. Just the mere fact that I chose to deal with certain aspects of this difficult season discreetly by hiding all evidence from you zapped the remaining energy I had. So each day I made up my mind that I would have to be calm and willed myself to be, so as not to heighten your suspicion regarding how far in debt we were. The truth was six months is a long time to owe someone least of all the Neurosurgeon who saved your life. Often times I wondered how I managed to keep sane as the thoughts about outstanding bills continuously surrounded me. This along with returning to work and focusing on your recovery took everything I had within me.

With God being one that is of perfect timing, I was not surprised that at this point in my life where I felt as if I was literally suffocating just happened to be the time when we were slated to meet up with my friends on the North Coast.  On our way down I kept reflecting on the conversation I had with my mother who pleaded with me to muster up the inner will to enjoy myself and make the most of it. I told her yes I would and as I journeyed down I wondered how on earth I could. My stomach was in knots and each time the phone vibrated my heart skipped a beat. The truth is as it related to the medical bills, I had no information to give. I know God was coming through but I just did not know how or the time frame.

The journey down was calm and serene, each community we passed through brought back fond memories of past trips we had together and after a while with the music playing and breeze blowing I forgot my cares….just for a little while. After a few hours after following the directions given, we pulled up at the Resort and took a few hours just taking in the scenery as everything was simply breathtaking. The lush vegetation, the flowers in all their bloom, the overall design of the building, everything was specially designed with the word "VACATION" in mind. It felt surreal almost as if I was in a dream, not only were we spending the next few days as the Doctor recommended at the seaside, we were blessed with an all-expense paid vacation worth over Two Thousand US$ Dollars (US$2,000)! I was so emotional about it all, not only did they chose Jamaica for their vacation, they were the same couple who had previously decided to let me keep the overpayment that the bank made in error from their account a few months before to assist with your medical bills. I even remember when a courier pulled up at our gate a few weeks after you came home from the hospital with a delivery from them. They had sent flowers and a gift basket filled with all the things you needed at the time you needed it the most. All of which they had ordered online from their home in Bermuda. I felt as if everything was divinely orchestrated for us and that gave me enough motivation to continue pressing during the wait as the truth is, if God is doing all this right here right now, He is working behind the scenes and is coming through for us.

Once we unloaded the car and headed for the condo we were welcomed with a wonderful luncheon that left us feeling like a King and a Queen. Amidst the talking and laughter, hearing the waves beach the shore and feeling the rush of the cool breeze; I was just in awe at all God had done. I kept thinking "am I really here?" And by just looking around at the happiness that surrounded us I was reminded of the fact that we are indeed blessed with loved ones around us who loved and cared for us deeply.

Having settled in our room we realized that the interior of the Resort was just as beautiful as the exterior. The views of the ocean and the pools were breathtaking, along with that the overall decor throughout the condo was one that spelled relaxation in its entirety. I felt as if I had stepped into a whole new world where anxiety and worry were nowhere to be found, where outstanding bills and payments were only a fleeting thought, a world that enabled me to focus solely on you with a peace of mind enabling me to relax too.

As we were in another location I began another routine of walking each morning on the seashore where we memorized words and phrases picked up along the way. There was also time allotted for games, where we learnt many card games and tricks along with doing art work. Pretty soon I realized that your Doctor was right as just being near the sea did wonders for you, it was as if the tension each morning dissipated in the cool sea breeze.

It's amazing how much we hear and see when our mind is less preoccupied with the cares of life. One morning as we sat on the rocks by the sea, we spotted a seagull busy fishing to find food. It was hard to miss this bird as at each passing minute he came closer and closer to us. Each time it caught something, it flew to a gazebo, watched, waited then zoned in for a catch again. I was amazed at its strategy and amazed that God always provides, even for the birds He provides. It was then and there I heard a soft voice barely above a whisper say "that is how I will provide and care for you". Tears filled my eyes as the Holy Spirit whispered those words of comfort to me and I sat there mesmerized as I watched the seagull swoop down for a catch over and over again. It wasn't the motion of this gentle creature that had me captivated, it was the mere fact that it was all alone, focused on its prey and moving stealthily with determination and expectation. It was as if it knew where exactly to fish for food and I was like God how amazing you are you not only provide but you led this bird to this exact location where it would be able to fish to his heart's delight. I felt so humbled as I realized how much God spoke to me using nature and His creation. The fact that He directed this particular bird to where we were on this particular morning spoke volumes to me.

It reminded me of one of the many journeys I took to the hospital to be at your side and one particular morning as I was driving, I saw the sun bursting through the clouds in all its glory and all the rays were focused on a patch on the mountain side. The view was breathtaking and once more I was amazed at God's masterpiece and His perfection in everything including nature and creation. That morning I was so nervous as nothing seemed to be going my way, I needed some funds and some serious funds too and while I gazed at the magnificent artwork before me I heard His voice saying "I will turn the hearts of men towards you". I slowed down and I looked at the awesome scenery before me and mulled over these words. At that moment I felt a weight lifting from my shoulders as I was reminded that I am never alone and that God sees all, hears all and understands all and that means no matter what, at this time He is right here with me.  As I remembered that encounter with God I smiled and as the seagull flew away in the distant skies I felt a certain level of peace as I related all that happened to what is to come.

The days that followed were almost divine, we played games, cooked, shared stories, swam and went out for dinner in the evenings. Few of the most memorable dining experience was at a Restaurant specializing in Indian Cuisine and another day on a lovely Pier. There were days when chilling on the beach and enjoying the scenery was all it took to remind me of just how blessed we are. Not only was I having fun with friends who would do anything to help me unwind, I was also having fun not as a widow but with my husband here as well. There were times I got nervous but not once did the phone ring, and as the days went by I slowly learnt how to relax and enjoy life as it was at that very moment in that very hour. Before we knew it, it was time to journey back home and although I know I would miss the resort, I was forever grateful for the opportunity that our friends gave us, one that happens only once in a lifetime.  So it was when we returned home we felt elevated, renewed, rejuvenated and full of strength and vigor. I began taking my prayer life to another level, refusing to be swayed, refusing to be denied, refusing to give up and no matter how it seemed refusing to believe that I am down and out. The more I began speaking and declaring these things in my life, the more I felt empowered knowing that my heavenly father, my creator, the one who parted the Red Sea, the one whose breath from his nostrils can burn a way through the mountains, the one who is enthroned on my praise, my way maker, is right here with me.  The more I realized the fact that God was with me, the more I knew that no matter how the flood waters came, no matter how I felt as if the waters are pulling me into a deep cold abyss no matter if I felt as if I was about to take my last breath, it would not overtake me. As God is my refuge, my strength, my fortress and He is the Lord who sits enthroned on the flood and as King forever (Psalm 29:10).

So it was, one morning when I got up for morning worship in the wee hours, my special time to engage in dialogue with my Heavenly Father, I was led to check my emails. This I had begun doing previously in faith, I would check my emails, messages, bank accounts and voicemails at routine intervals that I termed "faith checks" as any day now I believe God would come through and assistance would be granted towards all these bills. This morning as I decided to check I kept thinking, why check now? There is much to pray about before I returned to sleep and there was much to do in the morning after I awake. So there was really no time to check right now, plus this was God's time. However as these thoughts came bombarding in I decided to check, as if I wasn't supposed to why did the thought come to mind. Then and there as I looked in my inbox there was an email from your Doctor and the words I read were words I had waited for, for the past six months. In it he stated that your employer had come through and has cleared ALL of your outstanding major medical bills, he then went on to thank me for all I have done regarding follow ups and for taking such good care of you. I fell to my knees, my eyes instantly filled with tears and I read his email over and over and over again. God came through and He turned the hearts of men towards me as He said He would. I was in total awe not only was help given but help was given in the way I had asked God specifically for, which was to cover not some but all of your medical bills. I began praising and thanking God while silently crying as my prayers had been answered. I looked back at all the heartache, pain, suffering, embarrassment and struggles and thanked God they have now come to an end. It took six months but my prayers were answered and the answer was so much greater than many would have ever imagined. I knew with all my heart that there was no way that I could ever honor and thank God enough for all He has done for me, for you and in turn for us. Even telling Him thanks daily for the rest of my life would never be enough. That day, I decided to tell you about the other side of this journey of those answered prayers while you were out. The side that included the financial aspect, the struggles, hurt, shame and pain including the death of my grandfather and when I did tears came to your eyes as you could not believe how much it took to save your life nor how much I chose to endure all alone. All in the hopes of sparing your life and enabling you to continue on the path to full recovery.  Immediately we began to pray giving God thanks right then and there for all He had done and continue to do in our lives.  Not only were you alive, but you were alive, recovering well and the bills were paid without having to sell our car, home and most importantly without a pending lawsuit. Soon after that to my relief, the amount to replace what had been taken from the US$ account was also refunded. To God be the Glory great things He hath done.

God came through as we remained faithful in our deepest darkest season enabling Him to renew, transform and restore us along with everything that was associated and connected to us. In the twinkling of an eye our lives changed once more, this time in a good way. You were given another chance of life and we were debt free. With God being the God of splendor and grandeur it was no surprise that now was also the time when our prophecy regarding our children was revisited. The names you so easily remembered when you were slipping in and out of consciousness, in short order will be names resonating in our home.  Twice the love it will be! Hallelujah! God remembered us and to Him be all honour, glory and power. As I write this final chapter in this aspect of our story, I smile as the best is yet to come. God is indeed our restorer and as it is stated in Isaiah 32 vs 17, *"the work of righteousness shall be peace; and the effect of righteousness quietness and assurance forever"*. To God be the glory, He is indeed the one who answered all our prayers.

As we continue our journey with its many facets and intricacies called "LIFE", we continue looking forward to living each day experiencing those ***Answered Prayers While You are Here.*** Join us for ***When the waiting meets the promise*** as we encounter ***The Power of Faith, Hope & Love.***